Peace is a Doing Word

Prayer Patterns for Peacemakers

— BARBARA GLASSON —

Sacristy Press
PO Box 612, Durham, DH1 9HT

www.sacristy.co.uk

First published in 2022 by Sacristy Press, Durham

Copyright © Barbara Glasson 2022
The moral rights of the author have been asserted.

Sacristy Limited, registered in England & Wales, number 7565667

British Library Cataloguing-in-Publication Data
A catalogue record for the book is available from the British Library

ISBN 978-1-78959-222-1

Let the peace of Christ rule in your hearts, since as members of one body you were called to peace. And be thankful.

Colossians 3:15

It's one of those words—"peace". On the whole, most people think it's a good thing; we aspire to it both for ourselves and for the world, but we are not quite sure what it actually means. We want people to give us peace; we want communities to be peaceful; we have a vision of a world where people can live in harmony and with justice, and yet it is such an elusive word. Is peace simply absence of violence, or is it something that can be built even within conflict? Is peace something for inner tranquillity, or can we be positive influences for peace in international situations? Is it anything more than an aspirational dream, or can we both grow and live peacefully?

This book is an exploration; it has taken time to contemplate and write and during that gestation you will hear my own struggles as I try to wrestle with the contradictions and longings that this process and these questions have brought.

English does strange things with language. In the verse from Colossians above we read "you were called *to peace*". We can read this as a calling into peace as if peace is a noun, a thing to which to aspire, a future hope, but we can also read it as if peace is a verb, "to peace". It has made me wonder what it might mean "to peace", to understand peace as a doing word, and this has led me into a series of wonderings about how we could live a way of peace, day by day, evening by evening, in a creative and prayerful way. How can we embed peace into the everyday fabric of living, how can we engage in routine and life-transforming patterns of "doing peace"?

There are prayers and ponderings for each day, divided into twelve, four-weekly sections Within each section, there are seven thoughts in a pattern of waking, walking, seeing, acting, creating, becoming, reflecting. Sometimes these sections tell a story from around the world, sometimes the musing is more poetic or prayer-like. The section entitled "reflecting" includes questions that might be helpful to contemplate either alone or in a group. The rhythm and pattern of using these is yours to discern. At the end of each section are two further thoughts, "resting" and "blessing", in which I have imagined us letting go of the day's striving and relinquishing our struggles to sleep.

I hope this is a book that you will pick up regularly and often, either for private pondering or corporate prayer and worship as we learn together what it means "to peace", and I hope that in the process this transformational journey will also change the world—that's all!

1:1

Waking

The light is calling us into life,
into this life, into our life.
The light is here already,
ahead of us, yet to come.
The light is breaking open the darkness
with birdsong,
calling us, changing us.
The world has turned towards the morning,
we are called into this fresh day
which light is opening
like a book.

Walking

Barefoot,
tentative,
vulnerable,
I set foot into this day,
wriggle my toes
into faith.
Help me to step
into this gift
gently,
graciously,
peacefully.

Seeing

The optician recommends varifocals. This means that it is possible to see both close up and far away just by tilting the head differently. My father used to have special reading glasses for close-up work and a different pair on top of his head to drop into place for driving. Then he graduated to "half-moons", and then bifocals to skip between viewpoints. It strikes me that peacemakers need varifocals to distinguish between the near and the far away and to see them with equal clarity, tilting the head at different angles to change focus. Peacemaking needs to be the glass through which we look to see the big picture and the small detail as clearly as each other.

Acting

In the hills, above the settlements that spread across the valley, a farmer is planting an olive tree. His land has been in the family for generations; it is now deprived of access and water. In the valley, the white buildings of the settlement stretch towards him, menacing, pushing him, making his life difficult at every turn. Every building on his land has a demolition order, including the dog kennel. Yet he still plants the trees.

"I will not let them make me hate," he says.

It is the ultimate, gentle, mighty defiance. He will not let them make him any less of a man, any less of a Christian, any less of a neighbour.

Today, let me also say, "I will not let them make me hate."

Creating

There are some things that we feel called to because we find them relatively easy. We consider we have a gift and can take great pleasure from using it very well without struggle or anxiety. There are others to which we are equally called because of their complexity and intricacy. They are a challenge and yet also an imperative. Weaving is both things for me.

Weaving is both simple and incredibly complex. Its simplicity comes from understanding that by taking spun yarn, wool or cotton, hemp or flax, and lacing it through other threads, we will end up with cloth. In and out, up and down, weaving is a simple process of binaries: if you do this you will get that; if you go there, you will get here.

On the other hand, weaving has an almost infinite range of complexity. Warps must be wound in such a way so that they do not tangle, then threaded accurately through the heddles that hang from shafts. These strands are threaded methodically through a narrow grid or reed before being tensioned and tied without breaking. Treadles and shafts must be lifted in the correct order in accordance with the desired pattern.

The weaving teacher allows the students to play first, to get the feel of weaving on the loom she has already "dressed". They choose threads of different thicknesses and hues; they feel the sheer delight of the thump of the reed against the emerging cloth with the regularity of a heartbeat.

The next lesson brings more solemn faces, tongues between teeth, as they count the threads, pushing them through the heddles with furrowed concentration. At this point, weaving is unforgiving: any mistake shows remorselessly for the whole length of the fabric; any broken thread must be repaired with careful knots.

The teacher is wise: she shows the class the joy before the struggle, the possibility before the problem—but she reminds the class: it's all weaving; the painstaking threading as well as the play. Just like trying to create peace, the joy and the struggle. It's all weaving.

Becoming

Let us discuss two ways to cook a chop. Firstly, I can think about half an hour before dinner time, "I really fancy eating a chop", and so, hurriedly taking it out of the fridge, I wham it under the grill and while it is sizzling, I cook some vegetables and a sauce. Job done; tea made; chop eaten. It is a perfectly respectable but not very flavoursome chop.

The other way goes like this: I put the chop in a deep dish at breakfast time, cover it with spices and maybe some cider or other marinade. Let it soak up all this flavour until mid-afternoon, when I place it in the oven to cook slowly and gently. This chop will be deeply soaked in all the flavours that surrounded it all day; it will be infused with complex aromas, tender and delicious.

It's like this with peace. It's not something we can cook up quickly. We need to be soaked through with the intention of it; it needs to marinate our souls; it needs to infuse every part of our lives. Such a vocation takes time.

(Apologies to vegetarians, but I am not sure the analogy works so well with lentils!)

Reflecting

Let the peace of Christ rule in your hearts, since as members of one body you were called to peace. And be thankful.

In the Colossians reading, it says that followers of Jesus are *called* to peace:

- How do we think this calling is part of our vocation?
- Where are we called to challenge violence in our own community?
- What difficult things and what joyful things have we done this week?

Resting

When we dread the skulking wolf of hatred,
the dark shadows of war shiver us,
our bones ache for wanting,
longing, striving for peace,
stir the fire of your love.
Call us into
the care of your night watch,
lie down across the threshold of our fear
protect us,
beside the embers of this day.

Blessing

As you have called me into this day
so, as you call me into this night,
divest me of my anxiety,
fear and failure.
May I rest this night in peace,
in the company of the forgiven.

1:2

Waking

Daylight dawns,
like a forthright blackbird's song,
morning choruses
the insistence of this day.
Today is new,
the thrust of dew and twilight,
mist drawing the curtains of night,
calling me to step towards the light again.
I must step towards the light again,
I must leave the night behind again,
discern what is right again and again.

Walking

Walking is both the physical action of putting one foot in front
of the other and a metaphor for our progress through life. Not all
of us can walk physically, but we all change and move through
life in some way. Whilst the metaphor of "journey" is somewhat
overplayed in the Christian tradition because it can imply a line
from birth to death in which God has a straightforward plan, the
idea of "walking" gives us the freedom to choose which direction
or circle we will take. We talk about "walking into something"

as though it might have been a ploy to trap us inadvertently into something we later come to regret. We can also choose to "walk out" when through anger or frustration or a sudden revelation we realize that we are in the wrong place. It is in walking that we fall into step and into conversation with those around us and discern who we are called to become.

Seeing

The child sat in the optician's clinic with a task whilst her mother and the surgeon talked about her eyes. The task was to put the parrot in the cage. The adults conversed whilst she peered into the strange periscope, a high tube with two handles to manipulate the images. In her right eye the parrot, in her left eye the cage; she simply needed to make the two come together. It should have been simple. But one eye was lazy and the other took control, so when the parrot was very nearly captivated the overanxious eye took command, and there it was, that pesky parrot out and about again. She didn't like to interrupt the adults' conversation to tell them this.

Of course, if you could get the parrot in the cage, if you could get your two eyes to focus together for a moment, if there was no laziness or lack of focus, then something miraculous would happen. There would be a world in three dimensions instead of two; there would be a depth of field.

If only the one eye wasn't so lazy. If only the other eye didn't seize the advantage.

Acting

He was the minister in a city-centre mission. The premises were extensive if run down in that mixture of cultures that is any city centre—turn right to the business quarter, go left to the slums. He was edgy, difficult, didn't play the game. We had earned enough of his trust during the course of the day to be shown inside the church.

In the sanctuary, up the stairs, in the toilets, on every landing, there were people, conversing, eating, sleeping on the pews. They were refugees, fugitives, illegals who had fled over the border, to get away from the war and economic collapse in a neighbouring country, desperate to find safety and work. He said that there had been a number of babies born there, that the lighting often went off, that the conditions were precariously insanitary. He was beleaguered on all sides; the politicians said he was making things unstable; the church said he was making things political; the people said he was either doing far too much or far too little. For himself, he was not too troubled over what people said.

Later we drove some distance out of town. We saw a woman carrying a wardrobe on her head. We marvelled that she could do such a thing—we marvelled with our quaint white Western eyes at a woman carrying a wardrobe on her head. He simply said it was bad for her back, that no human should carry a wardrobe on their heads.

He was right; he consistently did and said what was right.

Creating

The act of creating is an act of the imagination: to create we must believe that something can come out of nothing, that something new can be born. We are probably led by an impulse, a question, a sense of the unknown, then by the process of possibilities, and then most likely by a moment of despair where the impetus of that first impulse runs into the realities of tangles or smudged paint or some other sort of a mess. Then, if we persevere, a further question might emerge, when we ponder whether this strange design, which probably bears no resemblance to our original idea, might not be put in the bin after all but could be worth finishing. When it is done, we set it aside, maybe disappointed or unsure, until later maybe we can greet it with fresh eyes, a nod of the head and we wonder how on earth that happened.

Becoming

The funeral director said to the clergy students that it was wise to leave some space during the service so that people could think their own thoughts. He also said that this was good practice, because it gave you a moment to remember what you should have done, to notice if you had left anything out, to collect yourself.

It's challenging though, to be able to leave space when we are so caught up with the event, trying to hold things together for people who are grieving, trying to be the one who is strong and trustworthy. Space feels like a crack for chaos to enter, for a mourner to cry out or an estranged family member to suddenly appear. It feels much better to keep going and get the job done.

Acting

There is a conversation going on between students around the subject of interfaith dialogue. The conversation considers ways in which people that cannot currently sit in the same room can be brought together, and how to manage such a dynamic, contemplating if this is even something to which to aspire. Could Ahmadi sit in the same room as those who think they are not truly Muslim? Can Jehovah's Witnesses sit with Baptists? Can Hindus and Jews and Muslims really talk about Israel and Palestine with open hearts and minds?

They are trying to be real within the complexity of it all, they are trying to discern what might be good practice.

Then a wise person says: "The way to bring peace is to be friends with the people with whom you cannot yet be friends."

Creating

I am watching the spider on the front gate, spinning a web. She is such a trapeze artist, swinging on a single strand between the crosspieces, busying herself with attaching the silk in intricate designs. Of course, she did this yesterday, and she will do it again tomorrow as we have no intention of not using the gate!

The spider is a reminder that the peacemaking process, wherever we find it, is only as strong as the connections between fragile threads. It also requires persistent resolve when it inevitably breaks down and needs to be remade; it is a daily task.

Becoming

Peace is so difficult. It is a concept to which most of us would ascribe, and yet there are so many annoyances and irritations that trip us up. Some of them might be distant frustrations that cause us to rant a bit at the news or the seeming incompetency of governments, our outrage at the perceived stupidity of those in power. But mostly, our peace is disrupted by those closer in, our neighbours, our children, our parents, our siblings. These closer-in people are our biggest challenge when we are clearly right and we have such a need to justify! What to do with all this anger, all this sibling jealousy, all this aggravation of just living? How to put this non-peace into some kind of reality?

Reflecting

Having a vocation as a peacemaker causes us to ask some simple yet challenging questions:

- How is it possible to live peacefully within "non-peace"?
- What are the points of connection where we can be strengthened in building our communities peacefully?
- How to be friends with someone who is not yet our friend?

Resting

If peace is a doing word, a calling, a way of being, then surely it is also a way of resting. Peace must come out of the balancing of things, of passionate activity and gentle respite, of resolutely seeking justice, relinquishing any sense of power within the bigger story of creation. There is the need to be angry, to remain angry, to be passionate and fired up and yet at the same time to let things go, to let ourselves go, to relax into the imperfect, unfinished business of living.

Blessing

In this night I ask to be still enough,
to hear the voice beyond the noise,
to listen to the call of my soul,
to pay attention to the deep dark song
of the wise night sky.

1:4

Waking

A peaceful way of life,
is my inspiration,
my aspiration,
my potential transformation,
yet
you call me into this troublesome world,
where hatred goes viral
and good people are silenced.
Shake me by my collar,
until I am fully awake
to the imperative of peace
in every aspect,
on every twist and turn
of today,
and every day.

Walking

The canal towpath follows the canal, not the other way around.
The canal is the main player: it cuts through from one point to
another resolutely following the contour lines, its sides shaped
by shovels, its floor poddled by navvies' feet. The canal is a

silent and determined courier: it does not flow with any haste; it allows moorhens to roost in precarious old tyres; it is only slightly ruffled by a passing narrowboat.

The towpath is its servant: it must follow the course of the waterway doggedly. At bridges, it must squeeze between the sides of the arches and the water's edge; at times, it needs to cross over to the other side or take steps upwards to cross a road.

On a long-distance canal walk, the canal becomes the companion of the day: there is no navigation involved, no map reading, no stiles or fences to climb; the canal is the only indicator of being on the right track, and it is possible to arrive at a wharf or industrial area without the first idea which town it belongs to.

Maybe it's a bit like this, trying to live a way of peace: the resolution to keep walking alongside, despite the twists and turns, the squeeze points and the lack of signposts. Just walking, trusting the process rather than knowing the destination.

Seeing

I write in praise of the humble chicken whose two eyes are doing separate things simultaneously! One eye is focused on the ground, the worm, the grain of corn, the passing grub, while the other is keeping a look out for foxes or other chicken-eating predators. What a class act! Being able to see near-to and far-away at the same time!

At the end of the COVID lockdown, there was a great rush to the hairdressers. Facebook was full of posts of newly clipped heads and smiling faces. This coincided with the return to military rule in Myanmar, the devastation the pandemic was causing in Brazil and India, a mass shooting in the United States.

It made me so grumpy that I wrote caustically:"Get a grip; get a hair grip!" But maybe I should have consulted a chicken.

We cannot deny the joy and liberation that the end of lockdown brought for our local communities and for individuals who had been cooped up for months, for whom a trip to the hairdresser's salon signified a return to some normality. Neither should we forget our place in the wide world where struggles and illness continue to disrupt human wellbeing. It's a challenge to see both the near-to and the far-away at the same time, to see and hear in three dimensions, but I guess if chickens can do it, I should at least try.

Acting

The two friends were talking on the phone, and the conversation came around to the challenges of still sharing their homes with their adult children. "I'm so fed up," one of them sighed, "with all the perfect children everyone else seems to have with their high-grade exam results and perfect marriages."

"It's capitalism," the other replied. "The competition around children; it's a symptom of capitalism."

The chat continued. They discussed how the aspirational ambitions of parents could be part of a capitalist ideology which said there needed to be competition. There always had to be a sense of getting ahead, pushing forward, achieving more, and this was projected into child-rearing. Our worth is measured by our success.

It would also seem that, if we are not careful, the idea of "vocation" can also be subject to capitalism; it gives an edge, a specialness, an ambition to personal achievement. And the idea of a peaceful way of life being vocational can also imply that we all need to be zen and tranquil all the time.

"Well, my kids are real, annoying and struggling," one friend says, and there is the laughter of recognition on the other end of the line, "Well, thank God for that!"

Creating

For those who have faith, there is an understanding that, somehow, we are created from the imagination of a creator. To create is to call into being, to have a vision of something emerging from nothing, from the alchemy of possibilities, to germinate the seed of an idea, to bring something new to birth. Creativity is a mystery, an impulse from a place unknown, an imperative to form something new and beautiful, something with a story, something pleasing or challenging or questioning or fiercely real. Creativity is primal: it is a calling to us from our creator; it is a vocation to live in a world of possibility and to dare to join in.

Becoming

Vocation is not a straight-line thing; rather it disrupts the straight trajectories and turns us on our heel. A vocation to peace is a transformational journey that reconfigures our very selves; it is a call to resistance, justice and right relations. Like a caterpillar that must completely reconfigure its DNA to become a butterfly, the call to become transformative peacekeepers has to begin with a radical reassessment of our priorities and the choices we make each day, both individually and as societies. This calling is an intentional process that starts from within, a call to dwell differently within our souls, and from there outwards to dwell differently in relation to others and to the earth.

Reflecting

If being called into living peacefully means a reconfiguration of our DNA then:

- What strategies could we use to see both local and international issues at the same time?
- What do we need to change in our lives to live more peacefully?
- How has capitalism impacted on our families and neighbours?

Resting

This boat does not rest on a quiet sea,
it is in turbulent water.
Stormy, tempestuous waves
wash over her bows.
We are restless, tossed about, sick.
Nevertheless,
we pray for a hammock,
slung between despair and fear,
a hammock to hold us level,
a hammock of equilibrium, of balance, of hope.

Blessing

May the imaginative voice of the insistent creator beckon us.
May the turbulent voice of the courageous spirit stir us.
May the quizzical voice of our companion Jesus challenge us.
May peace be our incentive, our motivation, our calling.

2:1

Waking

I know I might bump into all sorts of people today,
some encounters will be organized and in my diary,
others will be serendipitous or a nuisance.
Whatever way I relate to others,
whatever strategies I initiate to avoid others,
whatever way others impinge on my freedom or time,
I pray for the grace to know we are all one,
there is no such thing as "others",
only "us".

Walking

On the long-distance walk, there is a different rhythm, a different timekeeping, a different heartbeat to the journey. By contrast, on a single day out, it is possible to set off with pace and determination, to have a trajectory that is urgent to reach a destination. On a long-distance walk, there is always tomorrow to take into consideration, the aching muscles, the blisters, the resolve needed, the sense of instalments. The milestones will clock off each achievement; they are the time signature for the march.

Others find this difficult to understand. They come out with kindness to meet you; they park their cars at the furthest point and come jauntily into view, still fresh and excited. Meanwhile the long-distance walkers have hunkered down into the day; they are managing their sore feet and hunger differently. The day walkers have stories to tell, and their pace is too fast: they turn on their heels and set off with happy chatter. The long-distance walkers dig deep for politeness: they are content with the silence of their own company.

This walking community is like two oceans meeting, sweeping around the Cape of Good Hope, oceans of different currents and temperatures, turbulently joining and swirling into something unsettling. My hunch is that peacemaking is more of the long-distance walk, but it needs also enough grace to manage the day trippers.

Seeing

The government has a lot of terms for it—community cohesion, building resilience, levelling up, integration—but peacemaking is not easily described in these terms. It is hard to define outcomes, to fill out boxes, to quantify results, find the language to say that this particular piece of work has prevented a riot. For a start, communities are not one-dimensional: they are complex and nuanced and contradictory. There is no such thing as "a Muslim" or "a black person", just as there is no singularity to being white or Christian. Complexity is not something to be feared but rather to be celebrated. But the grant makers and the politicians want to quantify the outcomes of their funding strategies; they demand that forms are completed and deadlines reached. And so those that need the funding to survive spin them the yarn, concoct figures to meet requirements, collect good news stories, try to simplify what is intricate and contradictory.

Short-term goals are always about the next project, the next bright idea, the next reworking of the rationale, the need to find something new. Short-term goals are always papering over the cracks rather than bridging them.

If only the custodians of the cash and the makers of policy would come and be with us, so that we could point out what we can see from where we stand. If only they could look into the eyes of the people they would like us to call "service users" and see the deep wondrous complexity of our shared, messed-up humanity.

Acting

The office looks like any other office, a computer and some filing cabinets, a cluttered desk. The cabinets contain the searches; from the DNA of buried bones, the bodies are painstakingly, analysed, catalogued, identified. The desolate relatives are informed.

Destruction is so quick, the military take-over, the order of a dictator, the motorbike in the village at dead of night, the torch, the gunshot, the fire, the terror. But the piecing back together—that is not quick, the gathering of fragments, of data, of evidence.

This story is never complete, but maybe, eventually through this detailed work, some parts of it can be redeemed?

Creating

Even in company it is a solitary job. The breach in the wall must be sealed with the stones to hand, and each one handles differently, needs to be considered for its unique form. Don't choose it until you have looked at it closely, the work is too tiring to pick things up needlessly. The stone must be studied from all angles in relation to the others and the overall stability of the wall. It must sit firmly, not rock or pivot or change the balance of the overall structure. Each rock is gripped and positioned, pushed and adjusted until it takes its place; the new piece of wall must graft into the old. Sometimes an old clay pipe is found in the debris, a sign of other workers whose hands considered these same rocks. Sometimes a fossil or a piece of lead ore hint at different stories. This wall will keep the sheep enclosed, but it is a kind wall, a boundary, not a barricade.

Becoming

Some describe the Trinity as a perichoresis—a dance between the divine Parent, Child and Spirit. I like to think that the one God some describe as immortal and invisible dances with the joy of the life they have called into being. The God whom we find in different ways, separate and yet together, contradictory and yet unified. It helps, on days when life seems fragmented and we are trying to hold it all together, to think that this search for integrity is part of God's dance.

Reflecting

Let the peace of Christ rule in your hearts, *since as members of one body* you were called to peace. And be thankful.

The Colossians reading reminds us that we are "members of one body" and that the need for integrity and relationship is at the heart of our calling.

- Where do we see people patiently piecing back together things that have been broken?
- How might we challenge and change funding strategies?
- How does God dance in our communities?

Resting

If I go to bed tonight with company,
or alone,
whether I sleep with my lover,
adversary, friend, or stranger,
if I go to bed calm with myself and others
or upset with both,
whether I sleep with preying errors,
or pleasing satisfaction,
if alone I am my best
or beset with terrors
if in company I fret
or imagine hidden danger—
in whatever company of solitude or comfort,
whatever test
I face this night,
bring peace I pray
and rest.

Blessing

Help me not to fear the darkness,
for dark and light are both alike to you.
Help me to be embraced by the night sky,
enfolded in the arms of the Milky Way.
Let the light of the moon's countenance shine upon me,
the Plough turn the tilt of this day,
into fertile ground for tomorrow.

2:2

Waking

Shake away,
dreams that haunt our wakefulness,
terrors that remain on our pillows,
uncertainties that shadow the curtains
from the rising sun.
Give us assurance of your steadfast grace,
that nothing on earth or in heaven
can diminish our lives,
or your love for us.

Walking

The ants are making their way up the cherry tree to farm the aphids. They are a procession, determined and drawn by the need to sustain their community. Each ant seems to know both their direction of travel and their purpose: they are individuals and yet keep common cause. We may consider the ants laboriously driven creatures, but they show us something profound, as they make an orderly procession up the tree—that mission only makes sense in community.

Seeing

The sculptures on the beach draw a lot of attention as they stare out across the Mersey estuary in the same direction that so many migrants have followed from Liverpool to new lives around the world. They not only indicate an emigration across the ocean, but also bring an immigration to Crosby beach, where many are drawn towards them on their walks along the expansive shoreline. It is not uncommon to see people walking right around one statue to view it from all angles. Sometimes the sculptures are dressed in woolly hats and coats or football shirts, and many visitors pose alongside to take a photo.

All sculpture needs space for the viewer to walk around, to view from every direction, providing the possibility to inhabit this three-dimensional world and to marvel at the skill and insight that art inhabits.

Acting

Somebody said today, "The world is within reach", as if the world had somehow previously been distant from us. I reflect that the world is where I am standing and I have no need to reach for it. Rather, I can open my hands to it and stretch towards what it is teaching me in the intense, ordinary immensity of the exquisite present moment.

Creating

The farmer is cutting the lush knee-high grass into wide strips of hay to be dried in the June sunshine. Swathes of buttercups, rye grass, vetch and nettles slowly become limp under the strengthening sun. I feel sad for the inevitable destruction of this harvest, for the cutting down, for the loss of bloom and lustre, for all the creatures that rest and nestle in the fronds of the ripening heads of growth. Yet if there is no reaping, there is no fodder; if there is no cutting back, there is no new growth.

Becoming

I want to be a peacemaker, but people are so annoying! They say the same thing over and over; they don't listen, and they plough on with such disregard for others. I am not a woolly liberal or a God-botherer as some would think; I am a resolute and determined person of faith; I believe that seeking peace is not a weakness but a strength. Yet I know that I need other people in order to become someone of integrity and that I can only respond to injustice and turmoil within the company and wisdom of others. Dear God, help me to be more patient with the people who annoy me and who equally may desire peace, justice, humble power and insight and—although it is hard to imagine—might find me annoying too!

Reflecting

- How can we be peacemakers as "members of one body"?
- How could we, as individuals, be more aware of our personal views which annoy others?
- What pieces of art or sculptures have we walked around to view from all sides?

Resting

I am not sure what today was all about, what steps I took on this troublesome journey. But whatever I did, whatever I prayed, whatever I dreamt, whatever I shared, whatever I failed in achieving, whatever I forgot, whatever I diminished, whatever I withheld, take these things from me, I pray. Wipe the face of this day clean. Give me the peace that passes all understanding, passes all endeavour, passes all longing, passes into this dark and forgiving night of reconciliation.

Blessing

God is peace; may I reside here.
God is silence; may I be heard here.
God is love; may I be held here.
Together with those I love and those who are my enemies,
together with the closest ones and the distant ones,
together with the clarity of inspiration
    and the despair of regret.
In this dark hour, I relinquish the solitary me of self.
In this dark hour, I reach out for new connections.
In this dark hour, I become one with all
    people that are the heart of things.
Together we come, alone yet holding hands,
isolated yet singing,
solitary yet standing together
on this same, lonely, glorious earth.

2:3

Waking

There is a strikingly simple yet profound first line to the morning prayers of the Corrymeela Community: "We start this day alone." It reminds us of the truth of our own loneliness. We are born alone, and we die alone: these are journeys in which we travel unaccompanied, and yet, we do have companions, those who listen, who hold our hands, who cradle us in so many ways. Together we are alone, alone we are together. I ponder this as I begin this day, both alone and in company, both isolated and accompanied, both solitary and gregarious. My peace lies somewhere in this mix. Peace is not always found in the absence of others, and yet neither is it always found in their company.

Walking

It was in Florence she first saw the rainbow flag with the letters PACE, an emblem of inclusion and peace. In translation it means "PEACE", but to English eyes, the original contains a deeper truth, because "peace" and "pace" are profoundly intertwined. Time is not our master: it is an invention for catching buses and writing essays to a deadline; it is a tool. We set the pace; we walk the path; we are the metronome of our days. And circling both these words is the word "patience", that deeply transformative aspect of the pace we choose to set. Patience has time for self and others, patience digs deep, patience is the outworking of grace. Patience allows the spaces between us to hold the possibilities of peace.

Seeing

Someone unknown to me once remarked that "Under the sun, all the shadows fall in the same direction." It sounds profound but is it true? At the literal level yes, if we stand together facing the same light then the shadows will always be at our back, but at a metaphorical level surely we all walk with our own shadows, our own darkness, our own particular griefs? If we say all the shadows fall in the same direction, do we diminish the struggle that is ours alone, our own darkness, our own sorrow? And yet, there is a solidarity in shadows, just as there is a chorus of hallelujahs from those of us that embrace the warm light of the sun on our face. Maybe peace comes knowing not only the bright shining hope of a new day, but also the solidarity in shadow.

Acting

Faith imagines humanity differently,
it calls us to a raw edge,
to a frayed selvedge,
unravelling the tugs
of self-doubt.
Faith plays tag,
tapping us on the shoulder
and saying, "You are it!"
Faith says, "Go",
but not alone;
as we bump along
we will collide with
unlikely companions on the track.
Faith is lively,
loving, possible,
bringing energy from others
wisdom from happenstance.
Faith throws a bridge
across the terrifying canyon of guilt.
Faith dares us to trust the rope's tension,
compels us,
commands us,
"Cross!"

Creating

Hope Street in Liverpool links the two cathedrals; it marks a path of reconciliation between sectarian divisions. At one end the vast, red-stone, heavyweight building of the Anglicans; at the other the crown of "Paddy's Wigwam", the light, colourful pointed apex of the Roman Catholic cathedral. In between, a street of theatre and bistro, of tourists and revellers.

On the pavement halfway along the street sits a pile of luggage, a piece of art, representing the vibrancy and transience of this connecting place. This installation, comprised of stone suitcases, is the work of the artist John King, who in 1998 positioned this sculpture to represent the personalities and celebrities associated with this vibrant city. Liverpool is a place of many arrivals and departures, looking out to Ireland, America and beyond.

Nowadays, the sculpture provides a resting place for tourists and vagabonds alike. The flat surfaces of the suitcases offer a handy seat for the weary, or those with time to look around. The connections with the past and the present are depicted with engraved labels and leather stone straps. This simple yet iconic piece of art gives many passers-by a place to sit on Hope Street.

Becoming

The conversation that had begun in the early 1990s came in the form of draft resolutions to the Methodist Conference of 2021. Thirty years of debate, consultation at every level of the Church, a working group looking in detail at many aspects of human relating, a document called, "God in Love Unites us", scrutiny by the Faith and Order Committee, impassioned speeches from all "sides" of the debate, from international partners, from LGBT+

Christians, pleas for a return to Scripture from those who feared we were straying from the true path, pleas for inclusion from those who felt hurt and excluded. Draft resolutions and a vote, taken quietly, received quietly, with dignity, with a shared ache despite disparate views. An agreement that the Methodist Church will have two understandings of marriage, the first traditional view to be upheld, one man and one woman, the second recognizing that marriage could be between any two adults, the intention of both the understanding to live faithfully and lovingly with one partner for life.

The decision has been remarkable and courageous. But the astonishing thing has been the intention to live with contradictory convictions and yet hold together as one Church. Time will tell if this will be realized. There are people with strongly held beliefs that are both convinced that the other is wrong, do not honour Scripture, do not understand the nature of human experience. Imagine though, if we could hold together as a Church, respecting difference, disagreeing well, watching over one another in love . . . . imagine that.

Reflecting

- How are our actions in solidarity with others enabling peace to become "a doing word"?
- When has faith "played tag" with us?
- Where have we found a "betwixt and between" place to rediscover hope?

Resting

There are voices,
chitter-chattering in my head,
and the babel of clattering contradictions
clitter clattering, words said.
Tip tap of clipped mutterings,
pitter prattling like rain
pattering on a lead roof.
Let their power stutter
into the night's dark quietness,
stall their insistent muttering
as I go to bed.

Blessing

Bless all whom I love tonight,
and all I should love more.
Bless all the good I've been,
and all as yet undone.
Bless my enemies,
without and within.
Bless all your beloved people with peaceful sleep,
under the shared cloak of the night sky.

2:4

Waking

Summon us into this day,
pull off the sheets of complacency,
shake us awake to injustice and inequality,
shower us with the icy water of contrition,
give us a fresh, bright start,
insist that we open our eyes.

Walking

Two men are walking on the road to Emmaus when a third falls
into step with them. Their walk is a trudge of disappointment.
"We had hoped . . . ", they tell the stranger. They had hoped that a
new dawn was breaking, that following the wandering Galilean
known to them as Jesus would have borne fruit. Now they were
disconsolate, defeated, confused; hope had been crucified.

Curious then, in the circumstances, that they tolerated a
stranger explaining the scriptures to them starting from the
beginning, and even more curious that they invited him in for
a meal. Surely they simply wanted their own homes, their own
space and their own beds? It is not until their companion picks
up the bread and breaks it that the story pivots—their eyes are
opened!

Seeing

Colour is all about light, what is absorbed and what is reflected. Think of the many shades of blue—navy, sky, periwinkle, ultramarine, cerulean, azure, picotee, midnight—and these are simply the ones that can be replicated and squeezed into tubes of paint. Think of the blue of the sea, bright and sparkling, deep and menacing, tropical or muddied. Colours, like people, vary their shades according to the way the light falls on them, how they communicate the depth below from the surface, how they absorb the light or reflect the source of its brilliance. All these hues work together, blend, shade, give each other subtlety. Yes, colours are like people, infinitely possible, infinitely varied, infinitely beautiful and complex, blended uniquely by mingling with others.

Acting

Set the wild goose free,
hatch memories of the sky –
dare her—leave your brooding,
rise high above the sea!
Expand your folded wings,
extend your widest span,
freefall into freedom
let the wild goose fly.

Creating

In order to spin wool, it is necessary to clean and comb the fibres so that they lie parallel to each other. Then the wheel is threaded with a "leader", often string, which is tied securely around the bobbin. The leader directs the spinning to wind in an unbroken thread and the tension must be regulated so that, at the speed of the spinner, the risk of breakage is kept to a minimum. Once a bobbin is complete, a second one must be spun in the same way and then the two together are plied counter-clockwise so that the twist is neutralized. The freshly spun yarn is then washed and hung with a weight to pull out the residual tension before use.

Becoming

Maybe peace isn't a thing,
or a state of mind,
or an aspiration,
or a goal
maybe peace is just a space,
betwixt and between,
neither there nor here,
neither then nor now?
Maybe peace is the possibility,
between this and that,
between right and wrong,
between certainty and doubt?
Maybe peace is the maybe
within all the contradictions?

Reflecting

- If we think about two strands of twisted wool being plied to "neutralize" the twist, what relationships might enable us to live with less tension?
- If peace isn't a thing, then what is it?
- What was it about the stranger that caused the disciples to invite him in for a meal?

Resting

Tonight, I relinquish my right to be right.
I resign my position in charge.
I let it all go, release my grip, let the boat sail.
Tonight, I immerse myself in a deeper sea,
in a darker night, in a gentler light.
Tonight, I hand it all over into the vast, fathomless, infinite
freedom of unknowing.

Blessing

Between you and me, let there be peace.
Between here and there, let there be peace.
Between right and wrong, let there be peace.
Between certainty and doubt, let there be peace.
The deep peace of enough,
the deep peace of together,
the deep peace of sufficient,
the deep peace of friendship,
be ours, yours and mine,
here and forever.

3:1

Waking

Spacious love,
unfold this day
as a flower
in the pavement,
with all its fragile might
grows upward,
yearning for light.
In my pressured schedule
give returning spaces,
moments to notice the tiny things,
in danger of being trampled
by my hasty feet.
May I live this day discerning
the intense immensity of
your unearned grace.

Walking

The parish council has a dilemma. There is a waiting list from local residents wanting an allotment, yet old George has two plots that are overgrown and seemingly uncared for. They all know George, his eccentric, recalcitrant ways, his commitment to the bees, his idea of what is natural. However, the allotment agreement says that priority is given to those in the parish, and some of those have been waiting a long, long time to acquire just a single plot to grow some vegetables. George is stubborn and fixed in his ways and, what is euphemistically described as "a local character". But then, there are people waiting, different people whose characters are not yet known but who want to belong, albeit in a small way, by growing beans and keeping hens. Is peace a doing word, an undoing word or a redoing word?

Seeing

The way we see the world is intricately linked to the way we actually see, to our eyesight, to our vision. Those who cannot see in three dimensions, because of defects in eyesight, must learn this skill through trial and error. People with squints or astigmatism, who have double vision or only one eye, have to learn to judge distances the hard way, by misjudging steps and tripping over their feet or breaking precious objects when they cannot discern their exact position on the table. They are often thought clumsy, told to be more careful, not trusted with the fragile vase. Even though learning how to see in a different way, through trial and error, through breakages and falls, through ridicule and nagging, they maybe have sight that others cannot perceive.

Acting

The chaplain does not just offer sanctuary; the chaplain is the sanctuary. The chaplain may not provide a refuge, a place of hospitality like a chapel or labyrinth, rather they are that thing, they are the place of safety. Chaplains bring themselves, their presence beside the bed or in the cell, the space, the chance for a moment to step into something else, to be with someone else. The chaplain then has the chapel in their cupped hands, in their spacious presence, in their time to stand beside you for as long as it takes. They do not simply offer a place of prayer; they are the prayer; they are the buttresses that hold the walls of the ancient cathedral of prayer open to you; they are the apse in which to ask the questions that torment, where you can light a candle of longing in the safety of being understood at last. The chaplain is the refuge, the shelter, the stable, the hayloft, the open arms of humanity, in ordinary time, in the here and now, at the heart of the matter.

Creating

Struggle may not be our desire
but it is our heritage;
we are bequeathed it from our ancestors,
inherit our due share
sometimes more.
Complexity, it seems,
is an unanticipated route to simplicity;
to be wise is to realize there is nothing left to lose,
a perverse parting gift.

Becoming

The trees will sing,
the branches will cry out loud,
raising the sap,
healing the nations.
Spears turned to shears,
briars to walking sticks,
threshing thorns from
brambles of hatred,
watering saplings of peace.

Reflecting

Let ***the peace*** of Christ rule in your hearts, since as
members of one body you were called to peace. And be
thankful.

The words of the Colossians reading "to peace" can be read two
ways: either we are beckoned into peace, or we can understand
peace to be a verb, a "doing word":

- Is peace a doing word, or an undoing and redoing word?
- How can accepting complexity be a route to simplicity?
- In what ways do we see the world differently from others?

Resting

I am tired tonight,
tired of being tired,
tried, and tired of being tried.
Untie this day, I pray,
release this knotted tangle,
retie me with ribbons of kindness,
let me retire in peace.

Blessing

Bless, I pray, this incomplete day,
all that has been unsatisfactory,
let it be enough.
Bless, I pray, the mess and muddle,
the unfinished business of it all,
let it be enough.
Bless the niggles and confusion,
the loose ends, the unresolved desires,
let it be enough for now,
let it be enough.

3:2

Waking

Let peace be a verb today,
a doing word, an active word,
a positive choice,
in the way of saying things,
in the way of doing things,
in the way of seeing things,
our intention for justice
within all interactions.
Let peace be more than "no war"
but a positive movement
towards transformation,
in every small step of the way,
let peace be a verb today.

Walking

The email exchange was becoming more and more antagonistic. The language was angry, recalcitrant, accusatory. He had been copied into the exchanges with both sides hoping for his approval of their proven point. He made few comments except to advise a pause before hitting "send", to think again before lobbing another verbal grenade.

Seeing

Context gives experience different hues, as the azure of the night sky skitters differently on the surface of water from the copper refractions of the midday sun. Actions will always be held within a landscape of other things, other experiences, other people, other memories, and those around will have the hues of different landscapes colouring their actions and reactions too. I must remember this. I must remember that to live peacefully is to discern a spectrum of nuance, interpretation and memories and that to live authentically is to perceive this spectrum in those around me with eyes wide and open, ready to be surprised by their dazzling and perplexing beauty.

Acting

In the desert between Pakistan and India, a day's jeep ride from any town, a village man stood in the dust with his bare feet. His feet were wide, his toes were thick, his heels leathery brown. He had never worn shoes. He said he had grown up a barefoot boy, rounding up the scrawny goats and moving them to where rain might have nourished a patch of scrub or brought some thorn tree to blossom. He said he had noticed the little creatures, ants and termites that also scurried about their business, and he feared that he might accidentally tread on one of these tiny creatures and squash it. That is why he had decided never to wear shoes.

Creating

One positive action for peacemaking would be to make small safe spaces for honest conversations. Intentional spaces, permissive spaces, spaces where no one will censor a story or censure a mistake. Where all shock could be suspended, every experience is valid, every opinion heard. The theory is simple, the reality costly. The holding of such a thing would require a massive inner space for the ones that held it, but the result could be transformational.

Becoming

Decline the verb "to peace"
I peace
You peace
He, she or it peaces
We peace
You peace
They peace
I am in pieces
You are in pieces
He, she or it is in pieces
We are in pieces
You are in pieces
They are in pieces
I am peacing
You are peacing
He, she or it is peacing
We are piecing together
You are piecing together
They are piecing together.
How can peace be declined?

Reflecting

- How can we make safe spaces for honest conversations?
- What decisions have we made to safeguard creation?
- In what ways could our relationship with social media be more peaceful?

Resting

As the earth turns towards darkness,
we turn towards rest.
As the moon gathers her family of stars,
we relinquish our grip on this fragile day.
As the skylarks yield responsibility to the owls,
we release our hold on control.
As the planet finds her gravitas,
we resolve to do the same.

Blessing

In small things,
aspirations, inspirations,
neutrons, neurons,
sighs, sights,
capillaries, corpuscles,
life flows on in small ways,
one pulse after another pulse,
flowing into the heartbeat
of the night.

3:3

Waking

What an extraordinary thing to be alive!
What a mystery to step into each morning,
as this blue planet, my home,
turns once again towards her distant star
for light and warmth.
What an extraordinary gift is given to me,
even though the day seems complicated,
relationships tangled,
responsibilities too weighty.
As I open my eyes this morning
let my first thought be "thank you!"

Walking

Seeking to live in peaceful ways always needs to be relational,
with both humans and the earth. We are embodied creatures,
made of chemicals and genetic configurations. This does not
diminish our relationship with the Creator but rather heightens
it. We are not placed on the earth as aliens, but are part of the
same substance; we have been born from its red soil and one
day will return to its substrate. So, as I try to discover the verb,
"to peace" in the events of today, I am aware that I need to be

more attentive to my impact on the created world around me. I must manage with less and gladly discover the subversive joy of re-using and recycling what I already have.

Seeing

The micro-lens attached to the mobile phone has added a new depth to the wonders of the garden. With it in place, it is possible to look closely into the very heart of a daisy, to see that the yellow centre is in fact a collection of dusty stamen individually as bright as a sun. The challenge of photographing a bee, which takes most of the afternoon, reveals the delicately segmented legs, the dusted fuzz of the stripy body, the pollen sacs heavy with contraband.

Acting

The events that initiated the lockdown of 2020, sparked by a coronavirus pandemic, have shone a spotlight on so many things we previously knew but chose not to see. The inequalities between richer nations and the Global South. The stark discrepancies of opportunities in Britain as the privileged have secured their healthcare and diet whilst the poorest have been left without choice on either. The arrogance of assuming we have rights when others have nothing at all. Some have chanted "No justice, no peace", and we all must learn that it is the justice for others, not simply for ourselves.

Creating

When the dead weight of the day
seems beyond me,
another black youth battered,
another boat belly up,
another blaze, another blast, another bomb,
let me do one small thing at least,
do one small creative, defiant thing,
one gracious loving act of resistance,
let me defeat defeat, resist despair,
keep believing, despite the contradictions,
that peace is possibly possible.

Becoming

What then is a peaceful way?
In the rafters of the house,
the solitary spider slings her web,
each day quietly
mending its tears,
making unseen bungee jumps
from musty beams,
over and over, repeatedly
repairing the rends
with new silk.
Meanwhile the activist bees,
indignant with buzz and sting,
protect their vulnerable young,
imprisoned in dark waxy cells,
once only,
thus sacrificing their own lives
to defend the hive.

Reflecting

- In our peacemaking do we follow the spider or the bee?
- When the world seems overwhelmingly violent, where do we find hope?
- What are environmental challenges teaching us about the imperative for peace?

Resting

I have noticed, whilst sitting late in the garden during the long evenings of summer, that the birds sing a dusk chorus. The swifts, of course, have been swooping and swirling since late afternoon, darting under the eaves with breathtaking velocity, but most of the other birds have been quiet, apart from a kerfuffle of pigeons in the broad branches of the ash tree and the occasional expletive from the rooks. But just before deciding that the wine glass is empty and should not be refilled and the candle is no longer repelling the midges, as the chill comes into the night air and the lights in the house look more appealing than the watery glow of the moon, then the birds gather up one last rally and, filling their feathery breasts with moist air, they throstle a finale to the day. So maybe, just this once, another glass of Sauvignon and a cardigan to be their audience for half an hour in appreciation of their ability to sing a chorus at dusk.

Blessing

Bless the wakefulness of this night with musing,
the musing with remembering,
the remembering with forgiveness,
the forgiveness with whimsy,
the whimsy with smiling,
the smiling with nodding—
and finally—
bless the nodding with sleep.

3:4

Waking

It is not doing the wrong thing that is the biggest problem; after all, most wrong things can be remedied, redeemed, repented or repaid, rather it is not doing anything at all that is the issue. It is the shrug of the shoulders in apathy or despair, the paralysis of imagination, the inertia caused by distractions. Motivation comes from empathy, from anguish, from passion for another's wellbeing, from seeing when things are not good enough and resolving to change them. It is always better to try and fail than never to try at all.

Walking

She was a Christian in Bangladesh, and every day she went into the refugee camps of Cox's Bazar. As she clambered out of the bus and entered the compounds that were the home for more than a million Rohingya refugees, the heat and dust hit her full in the face. Here, where women, children, men and boys were stranded between states, without education or prospects, violence was not uncommon.

Her destination was a small wooden building at the top of the sandy hill, where she was greeted by the women who had found a refuge there, a place to sleep or chat or get out of the overcrowded environment of the temporary shelters that had become their permanent homes. She spent the day sitting on the floor, teaching them English, helping them to sew, listening to their stories, stepping round them quietly as they tried to rest or pray.

Visitors came from the West and nodded and listened and went away moved yet feeling powerless, but she went every day up the hill, trying to embody a little peace.

Seeing

He said that he couldn't see what all the fuss was about "white male privilege", that in his team everyone was equal and could speak out. She wondered about his forthcoming house move. Had he had to consider whether his neighbours would accept him or throw eggs at his windows, had he ever weighed up whether he should go to a party because of getting home safely, if he had ever worried if he would be pulled out for questioning at an airport and what were the power dynamics of calling it, "his team"?

Acting

If I throw this stone to miss,
it will have a single thread
tied round its girth.
Can you trust me enough to let
it roll unkicked towards your feet?
If you knot your twine to mine,
then I in turn can pull things back.
Together we could step away from the
cliff face of our own certainties,
tentatively suspend a bridge
over this rift between us.

Creating

She said, there was no such thing as a wrong note,
just a right note in the wrong place,
if that's the score,
we are all discords,
seeking resolution.

Becoming

He told us about the notice in her classroom which read, "Sometimes yearning is not enough". It was a quote cited to inspire the students to try harder, to do their revision, to apply themselves to the task. We must be activists for peace; we must be resilient and determined; we must not be content with injustice wherever we see it; we must strive to change the patterns of oppression that constrain the poorest. Yet sometimes, yearning is all we can do, the anguish is all we can bear, the longing is all that remains—no, it is not enough, but sometimes it is all we have, and God knows, aching is better than feeling nothing at all.

Reflecting

- What are the distractions stopping me from peaceful actions?
- What movement could I make towards another person to resolve a conflict?
- Is yearning ever enough?

Resting

At last, the noise of the day quietens, darkness shakes her blanket over the tired earth, the night sky plumps her cloud pillows and draws the curtains over the sun. At last, with heads under wings, crouching in hollows or stone walls, the creatures burrow down into the night. At last, we can relinquish the pestering of the day, hunker down into different dreams. At last, there is some peace.

Blessing

Bless me, I pray with an unsettled spirit,
that I will be restless until I see justice.
Bless me, I pray with a troubled mind,
that a heartache for fairness will disturb my decisions.
Bless me, I pray with a determined body,
that I will stand firm beside those who have need.

4:1

Waking

Help me not to measure life
by any standard
other than the rule
of peace and love.
Give me capacity
to go an extra mile,
turn another cheek,
draw circles of peace
in the shifting sands of conflict.
Help me not to measure others
with a straight rule,
a rigid rule, an unbendable rule,
an unbreakable rule
but only by the span,
of your open, accepting, loving arms.

Walking

He was alone in a wooden cabin in the woods. Although he was an ordained priest and a member of a religious order, he lived as a hermit. Many church groups visited him and sought his wisdom, which usually came with a further question. This particular group were campaigning to "Make poverty history". It was a movement for justice for the poorest of the Global South. He pondered, and then asked, "Does that mean making poverty a thing of the past?" The question caused them to pause in their earnest conversation. He continued: "Or does it mean understanding history from the point of view of the poor?"

Seeing

She had a phase of painting oranges. She shone a bright light onto them and mixed her paint, bright orange and white on one side and a duller ochre for the further side. She said that the oranges were teaching her about light. I wondered quietly if it was the light that was teaching her about oranges. Then she became fascinated by the space around the orange, the point at which it rested on the bench, the long orange-shaped shadow that undergirded it. She explained that it was the interplay between the light and the shadow that gave the orange its form, that it was the space around the orange that informed the eye that this circle of paint was in fact an orange.

Acting

He was an old rogue really, cantankerous, awkward, with a shotgun in his wardrobe that he never mentioned. But I loved him for so many reasons: his memories of the family struggles, his carrying of the experiences of war, his determination not to wash. Grief is just a measure of love, so I ache for his passing, with a shake of the head and a wry smile.

Creating

The loom was warped, the threads counted and pulled to give an even tension; the shuttle was threaded and ready to go. Her feet would lift each shaft in turn; backwards and forwards the thread exacted the patterns she had imagined. She remembered another weaver sitting high in the mountains looking over the Himalayas, with a similar loom but cotton instead of wool, each day making the patterns appear, drawing the colours of the landscape into her cloth. She thought of the patience to go on believing that a pattern could appear, that the strands were threaded in the right order, that something beautiful could be wound into a fabric that could flow out onto the stone floor from the effort. She thought of the connection between the two of them, across the time zones, through the back and forth of the shuttles, going on trusting that something beautiful could happen.

Becoming

When he was eleven years old and soaked in the righteousness of nonconformity, he prayed, earnestly and on his knees, that he would become wise. It didn't work of course, because life happened: his wife left him; the baby was his only focus. There were other catastrophes all around. Things didn't work out as he once anticipated. In fact, life was quite a mess. Then one day, late on, when all that kerfuffle had died down a bit and, leaning on a walking stick because his knees weren't quite what they had been, he looked at the horizon on a moonlit night. He mused that prayers were not necessarily answered with deadlines.

Reflecting

Let the peace of Christ *rule in your hearts,* since as
members of one body you were called to peace. And be
thankful.

The Colossians reading reminds us that peace should "rule in
our hearts":

- How do we remain committed to peacemaking when it
  costs us privileges?
- Where are the wise ones in our community?
- How is it possible to live by a peaceful rule?

Resting

So, it wasn't an aha of a day
or a podium gold medal day
or a full stop sort of a day
it was just a middle of the road
middle of the week
middle of the range day
mid-life, mid-year, fair to middling sort of a day
so, at the end of this mediocre day
mid-sentence . . .
. . . amen.

Blessing

Blessed spirit of life,
plough the ending of this day
with your furrows of forgiveness,
that all we sowed in anticipation,
all we nurtured in hope,
all that grew towards the light,
can be gleaned and winnowed,
harvested into barns
for the winter
and the soil made ready
for fresh plantings.

4:2

Waking

Waking does not necessarily happen at dawn;
it also happens in the dead watches of the night:
at twilight, at three and five o'clock
before the birds have thought about singing,
in the times between dreams and remembering.
Waking happens when aspiration collides
    with disappointments,
when longings career into disillusion,
when light is contradicted by darkness.
Waking can happen in dissolute times,
can be like birth,
like stepping into the sea.

Walking

The poet asks if we can keep our heads whilst all around are
losing theirs, this seemingly turns all of us into men, even
women! I wonder if it is not the head that needs to be steadied,
but rather the heart and this, in my womanly experience, is a
trickier call. Emotions, passions, feelings are harder to control
in the moment than thoughts. Thoughts have to enlist the
assistance of the tongue to be released, but emotions lasso our

feet and upturn us in an instant. Our passionate selves release the desire to fight or flee; they can easily overwhelm the head. Keeping peace at the centre cannot just happen in the moment when others have lost equilibrium, but rather needs to be practised day in and day out. Only then will we have it to hand when all around are losing their heads.

Seeing

The first time she walked around the statue she was impressed by the scale of it, that a human could work with such a huge piece of stone and have the strength to shape it. The second time she was struck by the detail, the observation of the artist that meant each facet worked in three dimensions. The third time around, she noticed the surfaces, how they were polished so smoothly, reflected the light so beautifully, how they made her want to press her lips on their cool surface. And so she walked around and around until at last there was an intimacy between her and the statue that came from knowing each other profoundly—the statue began to converse with her as if they were related.

Acting

She was their first born: musical, sensitive, exasperating. Teenage years were as you would expect, somewhat chaotic, and the chaos didn't abate. There were various relationships, various musical gigs, various absent nights. And then the chaos turned into something else, to highs and lows that made the whole family career into chaos. The need for money, the loss of jobs, the loss of a sense of reality. They all tried to stay grounded, but they all slept less, made up stories about her future that turned into disaster movies. Trying to find the still point, the oasis, the reason became more and more difficult. Keeping the peace within mental ill health needed them all to dig deep.

Creating

The potter is asked, "How long does it take to make a pot?", and as he sits at his wheel and watches the lump of clay be pulled and slipped into the exact shape of the other bowls aligned along his workbench, he replies: "It takes a lifetime; each one takes a lifetime."

Becoming

The discipline of embodying peace needs to come from a day-to-day commitment, a determined resolve to make peaceful choices. If peace is a "doing word", then it must run deeply into our daily living, a deliberate choice until such time as we are formed differently.

Reflecting

- What choices will we make differently because of a commitment to peaceful living?
- What are the challenges to peace in relation to mental ill health?
- How will we "keep our heads whilst all around are losing theirs"?

Resting

The baby abandons the day to sleep, throwing her weary arms upward above her head. She has squirmed and grizzled towards bedtime, resisted the adult's resolve to get her into her cot, their storytelling, their lullaby singing and their strategies to salvage a small portion of the day for themselves. Eventually, she relaxes into the "hallelujah position", becomes heavy with sleep. As she is gently lowered into her cot, tucked around and free to grow into the night, there is a collective sigh of freedom.

Blessing

For the blessing of today, there is thanks.
For the challenge of today, there is commitment.
For the struggle of today, there is resolve.
For the outcome of today, there is determination.
But tonight there is sleep, the blessing will be sleep.

4:3

Waking

What is this peace of Christ to which I aspire? Is it the silence of submission through sacrificial love? Is it the buying of time in conflict by drawing in the sand? Is it the resilience of love without retaliation? Is it the subversion of dominance by resolute resistance? Truth is—I don't know—maybe all these and more. Maybe it is illusion. After all, Jesus did say that he didn't come to bring peace but a sword. My morning prayer is to ask for help to live faithfully within these contradictions.

Walking

The car got to the checkpoint, and the three visitors waved their passports at the border patrol. The guide, on the other hand, had to get out. He walked wearily towards the kiosk where a soldier, no older than his son, played with a rifle. He presented his identity documents, shouldered the humiliation of questioning once again, as he tried to return home. The visitors sat in the jeep waiting. Eventually he reappeared, his shoulders revealing his heavy heart. He is tired of the occupation, tired of telling visitors his story, tired of the day-to-day intimidation. He pulled himself back into the jeep, no words, the farce of this border has made the point.

Seeing

I can see how people are confined, consigned to bureaucracy, how in their striving to maintain standards of health and safety, of regulations, of protocols, they cannot set us free and subsequently are not free themselves. I can see how this ties their hands and feet so that, as the directors or principals or executive officers of an institution that they had once wanted to reform, they are so wrapped around by the constraints of organizational risk-aversion that they are no longer able to thrive. Because of this the institution that they want to transform will also fail. I wonder then, for the imaginative free thinkers around here, do we hang around whilst they work this out or do we set ourselves free elsewhere, somehow, anywhere and if so, where and how?

Acting

There have been two main tasks today. The first was to input a lot of data so that the students I teach can access the resources they need to write an essay. This has been a laborious process involving a spreadsheet and patience. The second task has been to walk the dog. For this we went down into the forest, through the field of ripening oats. We were surprised by a solitary, silent deer and noticed the tapping of the woodpecker. You might say that I worked for this morning and took time out to walk the dog. Or you could say that the morning was a waste of time and I connected with what was important in the woods. Or you could possibly say that between the whole of this was a sort of completeness in which a balance of things was held together.

Creating

The young woman on the radio was excited by the possibility of mending old clothes. It gave her great pleasure to make one good garment last; it was beneficial for the environment and healthy for her pocket. The popularity of the TV programme *The Repair Shop* shows that mending things is a common theme, not simply to save the planet but also to save the story. Things have provenance.

Peace is a slippery word; what does it mean? Maybe there is a clue in the concept of mending, of darning together relationships where the threads between us have worn thin.

Becoming

I have seen so many good people crumble: the devout who saw their children abused by drugs; the prosperous who had their certainties evaporate with their mental health; the toned whose bodies were lassoed by illness; the atheist with shipwrecked certainties. I have seen so many shaken, bereft and out of kilter. And I have also seen those who stand on a steady rock, with salt waves of misfortune lashing against their faces and who, despite terrible adversity, hold fast. And I wonder what makes the difference.

Reflecting

- What contradictory convictions do we hold about peace?
- Is it possible to "darn together" relationships when they have worn thin?
- Is our society so enmeshed with bureaucracy that it is impossible to be free?

Resting

They had gone up to the flat rooftop to get some air at the end of a day of dust and humidity. India had assaulted every sense, the bright-coloured saris of the women who emerged from the informal dwellings to walk barefoot along the side of the road, the children tugging at their pockets asking for money or food, the fruit sellers hawking piles of mangoes and pineapple, the rickshaws, motorbikes, brightly painted, hooting lorries and the occasional elephant. Even now at twilight the noise of the city continued on the street below; the shouts of the rubbish collectors could be heard amongst the incessant traffic. Tomorrow they would catch the aeroplane back to their small green island, kindly relatives would ask them what it had been like, and they knew they would not be able to say because words were not big enough to embrace what they felt right now on this rooftop. Imagining tomorrow they could hear their families say as they tried to understand, "Well, it's a different world, isn't it?" And they could hear their souls responding, "No, it's the same world!", and they wanted to hold this moment with all its sounds and smells and confusions and not let it leach back into what they had once thought normal.

Blessing

As the fierce sun passes light to the gentler moon,
may all that has been and all that is yet to come
be soothed by this night's rest.

4:4

Waking

For all those who wake today with no idea where they are,
or with whom they have spent the night,
or where the bathroom might be,
or how to get there,
or who the strangers are that waken them,
or how to expunge the terrors of their dreams,
I pray for enough calmness not to panic,
for a sense of self somewhere at their centre,
for steady companions, even if unnamed,
to give them their bearings.

Walking

Each morning I pull on my clothes and take a pair of sensible shoes out of the box of shoes. The first job is to take the dog up onto the hillside behind the house, to let him race across the fields at breakneck speed whilst I saunter on behind. As I take those shoes and bend to make a bow to lace them onto my reluctant feet, I also make a bow of their frayed laces to tighten them. This bowing is also a sign of reverence to the one who made me to walk in these hills, and the tying of this bow is a prayer of remembrance for all those I love and to whom my heart is tied, who wake up to walk their own hills today. (I also smile at the English language's double use of the word "bow"!)

Seeing

There are two contrasting stories that stand side by side for me today: one is of a friend's daughter who has just got married. There are pictures of her and her family on Facebook, a large marquee in a spacious green field, the heels and frocks of the guests, the exuberance of plenty.

The other is of a young man of the same age, who has been sent by the job centre on two bus journeys to start a job in a warehouse, but when he got there, it turned out the job was only for a day and that they will dock his benefits for going.

How can this be within a hair's breadth of each other, that two young people can be so divided by the privilege of some at the expense of others?

Acting

If we are to centre ourselves on Christ, what should we be doing? We see in Jesus a human who desires to live within the rule of God to discover the truth of his identity, and this leads him to question the authoritarian regime of the occupational forces around him. He does this by embodying a resistance based on grace and forgiveness. So, if I am to centre myself on this Christ, I also need to return all the time—in every question, in every decision—to the parameters of forgiveness and grace. This is tough when I see the levels of injustice around me, when the richest trample on the poorest, when capitalism diminishes those who are already disempowered. But I am discovering that to follow Jesus is not to follow the powerful elite but rather to find one's unique identity with those who do not need to cling to riches or power to know that they are loved.

Creating

The sewing machine, whilst it might appear to be an item that enslaved women in domestic servitude, was actually, in its day, an item of liberation. The solid, yet beautifully decorated, Singer that came into so many homes during the post-war years enabled the female members of a household to clothe themselves and others and to earn a few bob of their own. In the 2020s, we have become accustomed to home working. We have come to understand it as transferring the workplace to which we travelled and in which we travailed, back into the home. For those women that could first afford their sewing machines, this was not a transfer of an already familiar work environment into their spare room but rather the means to become emancipated, a way of expanding their horizons and claiming a new identity, albeit in a domiciliary setting. In this solid, simple, functional and affordable machine was the possibility of revolution.

Becoming

King, prince, lord, sovereign:
these are difficult words,
these are oppressive words,
these are suppressing words.
Write in me a lighter poetry,
like dandelion seeds floating on the morning air,
like skylarks rising on the evening's eddies
like laughter, belly up in a field of ripening wheat.
Offer liberation from the prose that clamps a ball and chain
around the ankles of my soul.
Like a key, release me from this sack of words,
free me from the life sentence
pronounced by those black-capped judging words.

Reflecting

- How do we centre ourselves in lives of forgiveness and grace?
- Where do we see inequalities within a hair's breadth of each other?
- When do we need to remember that there is only one world?

Resting

If peace is to be the centre, then it is the fulcrum of all that pivots in the ups and downs of the day. Like children on a see-saw, mercy and mercilessness, respect and rape, starvation and obscene affluence fling us too high or crash us bone-shaken onto the hard dry earth; we career between euphoria and despair. If I ask for peace to be at the centre, it does not take that away, but maybe it gives a point of connection with the balancing point, a reference point where my feet are still on the earth and my hands can keep their grip.

Blessing

From all that struts and stalks and stultifies,
deliver us this night.
From all that tears and tempts and terrifies,
deliver us this night.
From all that prowls and plots and petrifies,
deliver us this night.

5:1

Waking

As I put on my clothes,
divest me of my entitlement.
As I put on my boots,
unshoe me from my arrogance.
As I button close my coat,
open my heart wide.
As I set out on this day,
lay on my soul's table
settings of hospitality,
for the unshod, the unclothed
the unwelcomed and the unfed.

Walking

Peace is not simply an absence of war; it is a way of being together which requires decisions to live differently with each other and the earth. As such, it is not a gentle word but a resolute stance in which our natural defensiveness is changed from a desire to protect ourselves in favour of protecting others and the environment. Because we will never know what we are achieving, because removing our armour might seemingly be an act of self-destruction, because there is little acclaim for this path of resistance, because it may leave us open to ambush by the forces that seem irresistibly destructive, to resolve to live for peace is not passive, it requires a strength that emerges from apparent weakness. The desire to live peacefully is a lifetime's work, the lifetime of the planet.

Seeing

The commentators at the Olympic Games build up the anticipation of the event, introducing the athletes and praising their performance. Just before the starting gun, they inevitably comment that the competitor is "completely focused". Years of training and practice, injury and recovery, losing and despairing have brought them to this one particular, fleeting moment. Their focus is totally on this and nothing else.

How to focus on peace, how to make it the thing for which we train and yearn and align every thought, without becoming obsessive and irrational? Maybe it's not a sprint but a relay, where we can go all out and also step aside and cheer encouragingly those whose energy surpasses our own. Either way, we need to keep focused.

Acting

The English Defence League was coming to the city that had so many memories of previous riots. At first, the decision-makers were frozen: who should take a lead, the Council or the Police, how to keep people safe and off the streets, how to avoid abhorrent racist rhetoric that provoked crowds to violence? Then, strategies were put in place, barriers erected, youth services took young people out of town. Tensions rose, the police changed into riot gear, horses stood in front of the gathered protestors. And then, from the door of a city-centre hotel a bride and groom appeared! What were they doing there? Well, it was their wedding day which they had planned many months before any hint of a march. They were undaunted by the events outside; it was their day after all; it belonged to them not the antagonistic mob. The spectators turned their back on the EDL to applaud the newly-weds, cheers broke out, laughter subverted spleen, peace surprisingly prevailed.

Creating

Create in me a quiet mind,
dwell within my spiralling spirit
as an epicentre of calm.
Give me courage and resilience,
gentleness and stillness,
an attentive demeanour,
a centred soul.
Let everything within me long for peace,
everything without me be assurance
of your grace and love.

Reflecting

Let the peace of Christ rule *in your hearts*, since as members of one body you were called to peace. And be thankful.

The Colossians reading reminds us that the way of peace is a daily decision to make peace our focus:

- Can we recall moments when peace surprised us?
- What strategies do we have for staying focused on peace?
- Who are our role models for peace?

Becoming

The word "becoming" is a combination of "be" and "coming", so that, as we understand how we are formed and shaped by our existential reality, we are also approached, or approaching one who seeks a relationship with us. "Be" is the passive part of the word; "coming" is much more active, so the word "becoming" brings together both a centred reality and an active movement. When we think about "becoming", we bring the two together, both the need to be patient and still and the need to be in a positive relationship with those different from ourselves.

Resting

I am thankful that at nightfall my bed, my bedroom, my slumber will be safe enough for sleep, and I recall that this is a privilege not known to all people. I pray tonight for all those for whom the dark of night is a time of terrible anticipation, of terrifying recollection or fear of violence. As I pray for protection for them, remind me also that my prayer for their sheltering is a call to challenge my sheltered assumptions and a call for a stance against violence for all people, for all nights.

Blessing

Bless those whose nights are for work,
who keep the dark watches
alongside the distressed, the dying or the troubled.
Bless those whose nights are for hard toil,
who in the middle of their labour
are anxious or weary or want to give in.
Bless those whose nights are for endurance,
who suffer pain alone, without the comfort of company.
Bless those who watch or labour or endure,
with the knowledge they are not alone,
even in this darkness, they are not alone.

5:2

Waking

If I imagine the world as peaceable rather than hostile,
and if I imagine the humans around me with good intent,
if I believe this day can be tranquil,
I believe there is goodness at the heart of things,
if I can find the "thank you" before the "give me",
and the margin of grace before calculating
    the margin for error,
then this day will be a peaceful day, a
    gracious day, a good day,
if I can begin by imagining this as my
    good and best intention.

Walking

As a teacher of pastoral theology, I can give students many theories about what is best pastoral practice, but in my experience it is the hunch that makes the pastor. The sense that someone is on your mind, that the thought of them is nagging at you, that you wake up wondering about them: these are the promptings of the Spirit. How many times have I been driving somewhere and felt I just need to drop by and see this person, or how many times have I just been signing off on the computer when there is a compulsion to drop someone an email. To be a good pastor is to listen to the hunches, the deep wisdom of the heart's intuition, and then, however ludicrous it feels, to act on it.

Seeing

Some days are just a patchwork of this and that, of demand and challenge. They seem to lack any kind of focus, they feel all over the place, chaotic. I wonder how to pattern things differently, not in a particular task or achievement but rather in a determination to centre myself on a particular point: a point of integrity, of resolve, of stitching it all together. To live peaceably is to see differently, to tune out the disruptive white noise of chaotic incidents and to turn up the volume on the connections between what we see, what we hear and what we do.

Acting

A colleague asks for support as she deals with a particularly difficult situation. She is distraught and at times cornered by the structures she hoped she could trust. The supportive role is not to take sides, even though as a supporter I feel it is obvious where allegiances lie, rather it is to stand, stock still, listening, leaning into the anguish. Doing something by being there and that is hard enough.

Creating

It is a conversation about seams. He says, after the disintegration
of his marriage, he wants to get back to sewing, he knows the
importance of overlaid seams, the sort he used when he stitched
his first tent. I ponder that we don't desire a seamless society,
where everything is just one big bolt of tweed, rather we want
a hotchpotch of colours, designs, plaid, twill, herringbone, as
well as the plain weave of ordinary things. We want a frayed
rigmarole of swatches—but also the tailor's skill to make the
seams between the pieces, to imagine that a garment can be
made from all these oddments.

Reflecting

- When, in our experience, have we been asked to "stand
  there" alongside another person?
- Have we ever followed a hunch and found the result
  surprisingly intuitive?
- How could we imagine the world differently?

Becoming

Between our hopes and our regrets,
is a table
laid with a white cloth,
a plate of freshly baked scones—
some argue put the jam first
others, unconvinced,
layer fresh cream
insisting jam will follow.
I say,
at least there is a table,
everything else
is only about the order of things.

Resting

Divest this day
of all frills and fripperies,
of all adornment or superfluous layers,
strip it of everything that has added,
stuff of complication, or adornment, or fancies,
or made-up stories, of something other than the truth.
Cleanse the day of illusion,
of make believe, or masks.
In this simple, pared back,
bare-faced place,
share with me the naked,
honest, wiped clean,
place of peace
some know as heaven.

Blessing

As I press the buttons that turn off the electronic day,
"save", "close", "log out",
then let the out-of-office message also signify
that I am here and now and real and present,
to the click of the clock, the beat of the
    heart, the voice of the other,
the turn of the actual day.

5:3

Waking

If the night has been violent,
if there has been the sound of gunfire,
or rape or bombs,
if the tanks are on the street,
or memories stalk like lions,
come, loving presence,
come into this crucifixion
because you alone
in this persecution
spread your arms wide enough for
any fragments of hope.

Walking

Most mornings I walk the dog up the same hill. He is so familiar
with the route that he waits ahead of me in certain places whilst
I catch up. Although the path is the same each morning, the
experience is always different. Sometimes it is wet and muddy,
sometimes a low cloud obscures the view. In the spring, I notice
the snowdrops pushing through at the corners of the steep steps
descending into the dale. Sometimes there are cows mooching
around the water trough. Many days are repetitive and familiar

and yet there is always something new. I wonder what it will be today!

Seeing

I realize that to search for peace
requires total commitment,
like searching for a lost coin or a lost sheep.
It seems senseless, in the light of a
     majority's apparent security,
but I need to see the world differently.
All that matters is held within the lostness of things,
all that matters is within the search for the anguished,
all that matters is not matter, rather
the exquisite, intense, lamenting,
void at the centre of life,
where the dejected, who are convinced they can never matter,
are held in a different light.

Acting

The township was so crowded that each neighbour could hear the coughs and conversations of their neighbours, day in, day out. There could be no secrets; if the children were fractious or the aunties and sisters gathered around for a gossip, these things were shared through sound-permeable walls. So, when a man came home from the city having slaked his labourer's thirst with cheap beer, and there was now no money, and in his anger, he spat in the face of his wife or tore her clothes to rape her or hit her full square with his fists, then everyone knew. But nobody dared challenge such an angry man, nobody could brave going single-handed to her defence. So a meeting of the women was convened and a plan was devised. The next time they heard his drunken voice being raised, sensed his fists tightening, knew she was holding her arms over her head to defend her face, these neighbouring women reached down their empty cooking pots and spoons. They banged the spoons against those metal pans, together with all their might in a wall of noisy defiance against the violence to their sister. They drummed those pans loud and long, they shamed that man together, until he knew that they knew and that he was ashamed. It was a bloodless, noisy victory.

Creating

They were a small cooperative, helping to preserve traditional ways of life but realizing that things needed to change. Even before the spice trade had altered the economy of the island the villagers had always been weaving, using natural dyes from the forest trees to colour their spun cotton. The issue was that the traditional way of extracting the dye from the tree's roots killed the tree and meant that the forest was being decimated. The cooperative brought in some experts from the botanical gardens to see what could be done—they wanted to honour the traditional ways and yet protect the ecology of this remote and beautiful place. The scientists discovered that the rich red dye that they needed was also present in the leaves of the trees. With some help to extract it, there was no need to cut the tree down. In this way money from the sale of the cloth provided a school and a small clinic for the village, and the people and the trees continued to thrive.

Becoming

We were not born to be drowned
by water or circumstances,
or to hunker down for shade
under branchless trees.
We did not bear children
only to wade upstream
carrying them above our heads,
for fear of water snakes
or snipers.
We only required a name, a place,
a cooking pot, some goats
or if not goats then yams,
enough homely things,
a place not to be drowned.

Reflecting

- In what ways could we negotiate capitalism differently for the sake of the environment?
- What acts of peaceful subversion have we experienced?
- How do we seek friendship with God?

Resting

It is said that sloth is one of the deadly sins, but the word is not quite descriptive of acedia from which it derived—acedia is a mixture of existential boredom, sorrow and despair. It was experienced by monks in medieval times as a desire to escape their cells or to be distracted from the spiritual life by the business of many tasks. Acedia is a failure to desire and seek friendship with God. It is easy for the Protestant mind to resist sloth by being very busy. Yet busyness itself can be a distraction from seeking friendship with God. How much time in church is spent talking about rotas and tasks rather than the spiritual life? Acedia is a failure to act rather than idleness, and this existential inertia ultimately works against peacefulness. So, in this resting time, as the night offers a sabbatical from the distractions of the day, be they busyness or playing computer games, maybe we can find peace in reconnecting with God as our friend in the space that the night offers.

Blessing

Bless all who pace the floor this night,
hold babes in arms or restless thoughts.
Bless those who stare at stars this night,
hold distant loves or shattered dreams.
Bless all who curse the dark this night,
hold angry thoughts or broken hearts.
Bless us with peace and more this night,
with constant grace, with love's insight.

5:4

Waking

As I wake,
I pray
for all in captivity,
in cells,
in refugee camps,
political prisoners, hostages, trafficked.
May prayers lead to action,
action to justice,
justice to freedom.

Walking

At precisely twelve minutes past five each morning a motorbike
goes past the front of our house. I began to notice this as it is
often a wakeful time for me, and then I became fascinated by
the exact timing of this journey. Who is this person who wakes
at precisely the same time every day to make exactly the same
journey? I began to imagine their life: it couldn't possibly involve
children or dogs or chickens or traffic jams; nobody could make
such a precise journey with those distractions on the way. Where
are they going? How many years have they been making this
journey at exactly the same early hour of the morning? What is

the story? Then I noticed that I would begin to wake around five o'clock and listen out for this solitary motorcyclist, and I noticed that once they had gone past, I was able to go back to sleep more soundly. I wondered if they realized they were listened out for from behind the curtains of a dark house. I wonder how I can be more attentive to the ordinary comings and goings of life today, how to notice more of what I take for granted, the things that I treat as the back story to the main event.

Seeing

The group of young people gazed over the valley. In the distance, the wide expanses of the vast Indian landscape stretched out under a wide sky, cascading the burnished light of the setting sun onto a range of statuesque mountains. From the valley came the sounds of children, the shouts of the rubbish collectors, the barks of wandering dogs, the smell of mud and food and excrement. "Look at the mountains," some exclaimed. "Look at the slum," others chided. "That is so magnificent," some said gazing at the horizon. "That's a disgrace," others muttered, looking down.

Acting

Show me what injustice looks like,
so that I can recognize it,
even with a full stomach and a full wallet.
Confront me with my own complacency,
so that I am not satisfied
when others are victims of systems,

stripping them of their dignity and power.
Let injustice distress me,
scrape me with shards of remorse,
sand away my privilege.
Give me a loud enough voice
to say, "This is not good enough",
even if it costs me
all I assumed was mine.

Creating

The wet slop of clay,
centred on the wheel,
the potter's cracked palms
pressing the turning earth.
What is imagined—
a bowl, a goblet
a plate for bread?
Who will wet their lips
at the rim,
share the sacrament of friends,
dip bread, sip wine
on a summer's afternoon?
Who will drop it
on the kitchen floor
and sweep up the broken shards
crying,
or discover it abandoned in a sideboard
full of dust and memory?

Reflecting

- In our experience what does injustice look like?
- How could we become more attentive to the world around us?
- Where are the captives?

Becoming

If peace is a decision, then it is also a discipline, a restraint to behaviour, a check on the urges and impulses that fight back. To decide for peace means a decision for a way of life that favours friendship over rivalry and community over competition. This decision affects every other decision: how much to consume, how much to travel, how much to participate in political or community life. In turn, deciding for peace will be a process of transformation for the soul, checking out motives and meanings, centring on gentleness and restraint, stirring up a passion for justice.

Resting

As the house creaks itself to sleep,
spiders spin, owls quarter the fields,
mice and ants carry away
the detritus of the day,
we relinquish our illusion
of being the pivot
of this turning world.

Blessing

Let us rest easy:
from all apprehensions
calm us,
from all regrets
free us,
from all terrors
protect us.
Let us rest easy:
for all mistakes
forgive us,
for all intentions
inspire us,
for all decisions
resolve us.
Let us rest easy:
from the past
teach us,
from today
release us,
for tomorrow
dare us.
Let us rest easy.

6:1

Waking

As you turn back the covers of the night,
so turn the tables on injustice.
As you lighten the morning clouds,
so lighten the load of the oppressed.
As you break open the dawn,
so break the hold of violence.
As you draw wide the curtains of the sky,
so draw into being your way of peace.

Walking

There are days when the calling of peace seems too hard, when life closes in around us, our enemies, within and without. Like the mist that hangs over the hills, like the grey fog of a damp November morning, like the smudged lines between the ink of the words, between what we wanted to say and what we said, then this quest for peace is blotched and unclear. In these partially-sighted moments, we ask for the courage to put one foot in front of the other anyway, to trust the process if not the destination, to walk the path without signposts, to keep going.

Seeing

When we see with our mind's eye, we can imagine something differently. We not only react to the objects and shadows around us, but we begin to understand process; we can discern a route between where we are and what could happen around us. This knowledge comes from the 3-D vision of the mind, an ability to grasp complexity and not be afraid of it. There will be "aha moments" in which we suddenly comprehend a bigger picture or see the possibility of a different trajectory, or understand what is behind the motives of others.

Acting

Conflict, antagonisms, resentments and disagreements are part of being humans together. Inevitably there will be friction as we rub up against each other. This is not the disaster. The disaster only comes when these things are unresolved, when they fester, when they become destructive, when they escalate. Deciding for peace, then, is not about avoiding conflict or denying disagreement but rather noticing the possibility of their destruction and de-escalating their entropic potential. Friction can cause a lot of heat, but it can also be a force that slows things down enough for creativity, growth, even for laughter, if we decide to harness its potential for forward movement.

Creating

She said that, in the light of the unfolding international situation, the church should say something, create something, make a response, make a statement. It was tricky. It was August, those in leadership were on holiday, with the partners who had waited all year for long hours for them to come home, with the children who had been kissed and left with a babysitter whilst they went to yet another meeting, with the selves from which they had become estranged by the stress and busyness of it all. Really, an international crisis in August? How are they supposed to respond or speak, and what exactly are they supposed to do, or say? How could they add to any discourse of rebellion, what in heaven's name could they create at such a time as this?

Becoming

The greeting "shalom" is often translated as "peace", but this can be to lose part of its meaning. The word not only implies a peaceful intent but also the desire for the wholeness and wellbeing of the other. This desire is reflective of God's intention within every interaction. In a somewhat stylized way, it is also found in the act of "passing the peace" within a Christian eucharistic liturgy. The greeting of "The peace of the Lord be always with you" has the refrain "And also with you!", and as such indicates a mutual desire to reflect within the church community the wholeness of God's relationship with the whole of creation and the congregation's intention to embody this within the life of the community. As we desire to live the peaceful way, the way of "shalom", then there is embedded in it this imperative to embody grace-filled, wholesome, healing relationships with each other and the world around us.

Reflecting

Let the peace of Christ rule in your hearts, since as members of *one body* you were called to peace. And be thankful.

- As members of one body, how could we work together for peace?
- When is it acceptable for leaders not to act?
- How could we live the "shalom" of healing love?

Resting

Temper the bronze sword of my anger,
with the cool waters of your wisdom,
so that the rage that fires me
will be burnished with kindness,
sharpened by love's resolve.
On the anvil of truth,
hone an edge of tenderness,
in the forge of courage
bend my unyielding will
into an implement for peace.

Blessing

Peace be our steadfast company.
Peace be our constant friend.
Peace be our dancing partner.
Peace be our journey's end.

6:2

Waking

Before I go online,
check my emails,
see who has been in touch
from Australia, in the middle of the night,
or tweeted an opinion on a hashtag,
let me first be present to the light, the air, the water,
my dreams, my hopes, my terrors.
Before the day goes online,
let me be present to it,
let there be a moment to align my soul to peace.

Walking

Today was allocated to writing words and poems about peace,
but then someone began flailing the hedges in the Dale, and the
noise was so loud and disruptive that I resolved to go and buy
a greetings card needed to mark a celebration at the weekend.
No sooner was I back, when there was a phone message from
someone wanting to come around, but it was better and easier
for me to go there, so that was the morning over. After lunch,
there was a visitor who came with us to talk and to walk the
dog and then stayed for tea. And so here I am in the evening,

having lived a day and trying to think what peace might mean. I think it means to remember that whatever happens, whatever interrupts the neat plans of the day, there is always a return, a call back, a re-centring on what was first begun.

Seeing

In the J. B. Priestley play *An Inspector Calls*, there is the spotlight thrown on a family who thought everything was respectable and under control. The inspector—it is unclear if he is real or imaginary—shows the aspiring and content family how their actions have led to the alienation of a mill worker who at various points in her life interacted with their needs and desires. The play is not simply about that family and that girl, but rather a critique of the class-ridden mores of a particular era. I wonder, if that inspector called again, where he would throw the light of scrutiny. Who would stand convicted of complicity with oppressive regimes? How might we see and be seen differently if we were similarly inspected?

Acting

As a Christian, I want to affirm that peace is at the centre of all that I aspire to be and do, because of the example I see in Jesus. But then I am aware that this peaceful vocation is not unique to those who seek to follow Jesus; we see it manifest in Islam, in Buddhism, in Judaism and in many other followers of faith traditions. More than this, we often see the quest for peace deeply etched on the hearts of those who have no faith at all but who seek to follow a path of justice and to disarm the hatreds of the world. In this we Christians have a minor place amongst those who diligently follow a way of non-violence, of community cohesion, of shared justice. To claim superiority is not only delusional but also to revert to a kind of colonialism that implies we know best. To find our place in the peaceful order of things, amongst the passions and protests of an alliance of kindred peacebuilders, is a peaceful action in itself.

Creating

Out of the planed planks
of this old tree,
carve an ottoman,
polish its knotted grain,
raise its heavy lid.
Within its sacred space
place secrets, folded in
tattered rags, pain kept hidden,
tears unwept, grief left untold—
hold them for a moment, then
with thanks, when ready,
lay them down
within that dark and kindly
sanctuary.

Becoming

People want to be able to go to work, to educate their children, to serve a modest dinner. War is the disruption of this desire; it is the violent interruption, the catastrophic disintegration of the stability of ordinary life. Most humans want peace, and for most of the time, the peaceful times, there is space enough to flourish, to grow, to create, to cultivate the kind of society or civilization that they desire. If we were not mostly at peace, then humanity would not have created great things in the arts or culture or science or economic advance. Peace is the most ordinary of things. It is violence that is strange.

Reflecting

- What can we learn about peacemaking from traditions other than our own?
- If the inspector came knocking, what might he discover?
- How can we find strategies for peace when our lives are disrupted?

Resting

Shades are drawn,
shadows lengthen,
doors nudged closed,
peace in grades of grey,
in charcoal smudge,
in pencil's blunted blur,
sketched in the rub
and fudge of
what has etched today.

Blessing

Bless us with inner peace.
Bless us with outer peace.
Give us an active peace.
Give us creative peace.
Bless us within with peace.
Bless us without with peace.

6:3

Waking

Nourish the spirit of peace in me, I pray, today.
Root my feet in the soil of justice,
nurture the tender seeds of resistance,
weed out everything preventing the flourishing of others.
Nourish the spirit of peace in me,
I pray, today.

Walking

According to the Gospel of John, Jesus says that he is leaving his peace with the disciples after he has been crucified, not as the world gives but as his heavenly Father gives. Of all the bequests ever given, this is the most ambiguous and poignant. We may want to use the phrase "Rest in peace" for the deceased, but in this reversal of roles Jesus asks those left behind to inherit a legacy of peace from the one who has died, a peace beyond understanding, a peace that is otherworldly, a peace that defies the conventions of grief and certainty and points to a new relationship between earth and heaven. This is our inheritance, an inheritance of mysterious, deep, unfathomable, inexplicable, incarnate, holy, peaceful possibility.

Seeing

There is a perspective in understanding history that says the wars are the key points; that is why we learn their dates and times in chronological history, why we are quizzed about battles in exams, why we need to remember who won. Yet in doing so we glorify the narrative of war, antagonism and violence more than telling and honouring the stories of peace. Peace is an understated, unrecognized hero; peace is not the interlude between wars but rather the place of the ordinary, redemptive, everyday unspectacular healing of the world. In a world that values celebrity and drama and crisis and angst, then this kind of ordinary unsung peace is the source of our silent redemption.

Acting

Active peace is not the same as pacifism. Active peace demands positive, proactive, defiant steps in the opposite direction from warfare. To de-escalate violence, to step between people that are daggers drawn, to carve out space for negotiation, for conciliation, for seeing a situation with fresh eyes, is an intentional and costly action. Active peace is a proactive, deliberate step in the opposite direction from aggression.

Creating

It is a puzzle why God is so often described as an all-powerful Lord, a conqueror to be glorified, a warrior to be feared, when the first thing we hear within the biblical story is that God is the creator. Not an impersonal, violent creator, but one that starts with a conversation, with a pattern that spins out over time. Creation begins with a delirious dance of colour, light and shade, water and air, an imaginative kaleidoscope of variety, and most importantly with relationship—a good relationship between the creator, humanity and the whole earth. We are told, first off, that good relationship is at the heart of God's intention for the earth and its people. Seeking to restore peace, then, should be at the heart of our creative selves, should be at the heart of our relationship with creation.

Becoming

War is neither endless nor inevitable. Peace is not simply the interlude between wars but rather the way things should be. History shows that war rarely solves anything; it costs both financially and in the severing of human relationships, it is environmentally destructive and potentially catastrophic. War need not be. Resisting the rhetoric that justifies conflict is not a soft option but rather a powerful and essential prerogative for every human that desires ordinary daily affirmation and the flourishing of life.

Reflecting

- Where do we observe the rhetoric of war overpowering the stories of peace?
- What images of God help us to understand peaceful relationships?
- How could we be proactive for peace in our communities?

Resting

Be the leaven in my imagination,
so that when all is dead loss,
I will be lifted.
Be the kneading of my dreary thoughts,
the shaping of hope,
pounding pain into possibility.
Be the waiting within me,
so that slowly, patiently,
I will rise, transformed.

Blessing

In the certainty of your peace,
may we shelter in night's amnesty.
Inside the surety of your grace,
may we find safe sanctuary.
Within the security of your love,
may we unearth eternity.

6:4

Waking

Let me put on the whole armour of peace:
the hard hat of perseverance;
the belt of patience;
the work shoes of resilience;
the overalls of love.
Zip me into an attitude of listening,
button me into a resolve for equality,
fasten me into the high viz vest of justice,
put the spanner of questions in my hand,
the wooden spoon of resistance in my belt,
the pen of protest in my pocket!

Walking

Intuition and peace go hand in hand. The reading of a situation
in such a way as to anticipate next steps, and then to find a
strategy to defuse those steps is an act of discernment that runs
ahead of the career path of antagonism. Seeing the possibilities,
disarming the consequences in a firing range of potential targets,
taking the tinder from the hammer blows so the sparks do not
inflame the situation, that is the role of the peace prophet. Those
who run ahead and dampen the ammunition, who take the

hand-grenade that seemingly justifies revenge and throw it into the quarry of reasonable doubt—those who anticipate the points of ignition and pour the waters of reason on them or distract the protagonists with a wider vision for saving face—they are the ones who win.

Seeing

The picture is of a child, a girl, maybe five or six years old, wearing dark tunic and trousers. She is being passed from hand to hand up over a wall. The men are hauling her up, passing her between them towards the top; one man stands on the ground, stretching his arms, the other reaches over the top to grab her hands. Where are her mother, her siblings? Is one of these men her father, her uncle, her grandad? Who has their arms raised on the other side to catch her descent, anyone she knows? She is being lifted out of the gunfire, and lifted into what, an airport under siege, another checkpoint? I wonder where and with whom and if ever she will find peace.

Acting

In the harsh face of zero-hours contracts, of mindless warehouse jobs, of being another commodity on the production line of materialism, what right has anyone to demand of another human that they are peacemakers? Peacemaking seems a middle-class luxury for the financially secure and the powerfully replete. Righteous anger drives the dispossessed, but where to put that anger without turning into depression, hopelessness, anarchy? Acting for peace must start with acting for justice. Acting for justice means finding enough energy in the middle of all this disillusion to imagine that there is something else worth striving for than this relentless existence and for believing, despite all the evidence, that this might be possible.

Creating

Cities of musk and sorrow,
villages of absence and regret,
what will you conjure from this cauldron
of silence and desire?
Can we find peace in your fortified walls,
or justice in your paddocks?
In the trivia of everyday memories,
in the history of fortifications and defences,
will there be peace, could there be tranquillity?
Lead the flock through the gates of the city,
the armies to a field outside the barricades
where, hunkering down on the hillside,
between city and pasture, they unearth understanding.
In the cracks between highway and footpath
sow an alchemy of wildflowers.

Reflecting

- Do peace and justice always go hand in hand?
- How do we respond to images of children in warfare?
- When and how have we defused angry situations in peaceful ways?

Becoming

For those entrenched in battles, who act as turnkey in locked-in grievance, who are protagonists in conflict or besieged by the rhetoric of force, we pray for another language, another choice. For those who plunder the birthright of the powerless, who disenfranchise, humiliate or belittle the voiceless, whose wrath hinges on vengeance, we pray for another perspective, another option. For those who are intent on treachery, corruption or through strategy or legalism belittle or humiliate others, we pray for another discourse, another vision. Let the choices we make shape who we become, and our becoming be for integrity, diplomacy, forbearance, peace.

Resting

When the heft and heave of life
weigh us down,
when we are left carrying too much,
plodding our muddied hoof prints into
unforgiving furrows of the day,
bearing burdens that cannot be shed at nightfall, then
lift the grievance and gravity of this load,
not so that we are free of responsibilities,
on the contrary,
so that we can balance the yoke we are bearing
more evenly across our shoulders,
so that we can carry this weight differently.

Blessing

Into this night we meander,
stragglers and strugglers,
carefree, care-full,
trouble free, troublesome,
victims, vicious,
complacent, complicit,
here we come, a faltering,
company of vagabonds,
asking for your solace,
gracious companion,
compassionate Christ.

7:1

Waking

We wake with headlines
of catastrophes, carnage,
chaos, conflict.
We wake with the tabloid
typeface of terrors and terrorists.
How to interpret the column inches,
read between the lines of rhetoric,
know that this prose skims the
surface of the real story?
How to live within the complexity of the news
posing as truth?

Walking

The Hebrew that is translated "Prince of Peace" contains a deeper meaning. The word has contained within it the idea of "struggle", so that our understanding of a peaceful prince, found in Isaiah 9:6 and used by Christians in relation to Jesus, is also a "struggling prince". The path of peace was never an easy one, and it was never promised as such; the struggle is part of the process. Peace has always been a doing word!

Seeing

The project was called "Extraordinary Drawers", which caused a snigger and some curiosity! The idea was to take a photo of the contents of a drawer in your house or garden that represented something of your life, interests, faith and passions. You were invited to write a simple paragraph about the objects in the drawer. The resultant snaps were astonishing. One had a baby's little cardigan and an intravenous canular; the baby had needed a full blood change and that was the needle that had saved his life. One drawer was full of artefacts that illustrated the couple's identities as both Jewish and Japanese. One picture was of a drawer full of vibrantly coloured headscarves owned by a Sikh woman to make her turbans, another was full of "useful bits" that a man had stashed away, batteries, rubber bands, paperclips. So it went on, each drawer revealing something of ordinary life in all its rich complexity and nuance. The photos made a colourful exhibition at the National Media Museum in Bradford, but it also gave an unexpectedly quizzical insight into a delightful variety of hybrid histories and hidden stories.

Acting

The impulse for peace is provoked by violence. There can be no peace without first acknowledging that there is violence, bloodshed, pain, destruction. The height of peace must mirror the depth of violence; the intensity of one matches the intensity of the other. So, to be agents of peace, we must bear witness to the sumps of violent destruction. There is no easy peace, only the shore reached in the struggle to emerge from trauma and disintegration.

Creating

They received a small grant from the City Council to make something to mark the Tour de France bicycle race coming through the city. They said they would "knit a bridge" and true to their promise people knitted hundreds of woollen strips which, when held together by sturdy rope, was slung between the trees in the local park. Preceded by police vehicles and motorbikes, the hooting of horns and sirens, the hype of a big event, the bicycles zipped past in twenty seconds. It is doubtful if any of the riders noticed the bridge. However, in the park people were asking, "Who are you, why have you knitted a bridge?", and they were able to share a little of the work they did in the community, in interfaith dialogue, in offering hospitality to refugees. Later the knitting was made into blankets for people who needed to keep warm.

Becoming

She is a small elderly lady, slightly unsteady on her feet. As she enters the room, there is a tangible respect for her presence. She is a leader amongst the women who search for the Disappeared and who continue to demonstrate for political reform in Argentina. She talks quietly but with passion. She has heard so many stories from the mothers and grandmothers whose children were taken. She has heard so many unfinished stories of searches for those babies who may or may not have been adopted by American families, who may or may not be alive, who may or may not have children, even grandchildren, of their own. She has marched every week in the Plaza de Mayo, Buenos Aires. She has made speeches; she has inspired many to struggle for social and political change. She is frustrated by being old when there is so much more that needs to be done, yet she has become, through all this resolve and heartache, so much more than a small, elderly lady, slightly unsteady on her feet.

Reflecting

> Let the peace of Christ rule in your hearts, since as members of one body you were **called to peace**. And be thankful.

The Colossians reading calls us into "doing peace" and implies that this is not only vocation but struggle.

- Where have we seen sacrificial action for justice?
- When has something on the edge of the event caused something different to happen?
- How can we live a pattern of radical hospitality?

Resting

For safety reasons, they had been moved to a hotel rather than staying in the bishop's house. The country was on high alert after the assassination of a member of parliament; all Westerners were both a danger and in danger. The air was humid. The noise of taxis, the slow rotation of the creaking ceiling fan, the rattle of the faltering air-conditioning, the anxiety about kidnap all conspired against sleep. They decided to wear their clothes, "If I am going to be kidnapped, I am not going in my nightdress!" one said defiantly. The other had pushed the small fridge against the inside of the hotel room door, "At least we'll have a moment before the break in," she said. Fully clothed and sweltering they lay on their individual beds, listening to the noises of the night, talking to each other about one thing and another. Then one unrolled her prayer mat and, facing somewhere towards Mecca, said her prayers. The other pulled her Bible from her suitcase and, propped by pillows, also prayed. When they had both finished, they turned towards each other and laughed out loud at their futile resistance to what was going on around them, and the tiny fridge as their only means of defence. They put on their night clothes and slept remarkably soundly.

Blessing

Wise creator,
give us the wisdom,
loving Jesus
give us the compassion,
dancing spirit,
give us the imagination,
to live peaceably
within communities,
between nations,
inside ourselves.

7:2

Waking

For all who have slept on pavements,
park benches, cardboard boxes,
under leaking roofs,
we pray.
In this remembering,
stir us to activism,
lobbying, protest,
reform.

Walking

We tell the students that to be an ordained minister is a marathon and not a sprint, and they nod and write it down in their journals. Even so, they always set off too fast and are very soon out of breath, winded, tired or disillusioned. Partly, it is not their fault: they enter their churches bright-eyed and enthusiastic with ideas for change and energy, but their diaries have already been filled with the routine meetings and expectations that they have inherited from their predecessor. It is very hard to walk if the treadmill is already running at double speed.

Seeing

It was such a disappointment that the desert was not silent. Even when the group stopped talking and the engine of the jeep was turned off, even when they moved into their own space and tried to listen to the language of their own souls, the wind continued stirring the dust and buffeting their faces. At their feet, the sand and minerals of the Atacama Desert eddied and glinted. Chips of blue, sparkles of black, sharp pieces of silver stones hinting at the rich, plundered resource of the seemingly empty waste. It wasn't just the wind that disturbed the atmosphere; it was the sadness of the indentured labourers who had been paid with tokens that must be spent in the company shop; it was the scars on the landscape formed by the ruthless raiding of the mining companies; there was the churning of the stories, their own and others', that meant the desert could not be, of itself, a peaceful place.

Acting

He drove out into the townships where the people were expecting him to come. He made his way to a simple building, without walls but with a corrugated iron roof, where already there was singing. He sat, as he had done so many times before, on a wooden bench in front of a gathering of people cross-legged on the ground. Someone, a woman in a blue cotton dress, stood up and introduced him, "This is the bishop; he is here to listen to us." The singing continued for some time and then an elderly woman rose to her feet, "The jeep came late at night; they rounded up my son and put him in the back; he was shouting out; he was afraid . . . I went to the police station, but I could not find him . . . they ran backwards over his body in their vehicle . . . ."

He sat; he listened; he shook his head; he had heard it all before, and yet it was the first time. He offered no explanation, no excuse, no apology, no answer, he just listened. And then the singing began again, and as he drove away he could still hear it.

Creating

Upstairs, above a Bethlehem street, they sat to sew. Muslim women, Jewish women, Christian women, stitching patterns, making cushions and mats. They smiled with modest pride at their creations, deep red and orange threads criss-crossing into the loosely held canvas, designs passed down through many generations. Outside in the street was the turmoil of tourists, taxis, street vendors, but in this crowded room, perched modestly on plastic chairs, they made beautiful designs and conversations.

Becoming

Maybe we have thought too much of "becoming" as a personal, individual thing at the expense of community. To become a community requires compromise, self-sacrifice, negotiation, flexibility; it is not so much about the aspirations of an individual but the broader wellbeing of the whole. The quest for human rights is crucial, but to prioritize the rights of one person over the wellbeing of a whole community has the potential to harm both.

Reflecting

- Have we thought of "becoming" more as an individual endeavour than a community exercise?
- When have we experienced intentional listening to traumatic events?
- How could we pace our lives more evenly?

Resting

She suggested there should be a sabbath in every day, a period of time where we could stand back from the routines of toil or study and focus on other things, like the Benedictine monks having patterns of work and rest, of study and gardening, of walking and labouring. We so often store up our emotions, struggles, inner landscape until we feel there is time, a weekend, a holiday to deal with them. This practice has a habit of wrecking weekends and holidays! A sabbatical in every day, in which it is possible to be centred on peace, to restore body and soul, to reconnect with nature, seems like a healthier option, but will take practice.

Blessing

As we release the clutches of this day,
as the shadows lengthen,
dusk settles over the fields and pavements,
streetlamps take over from the sun,
lights dim on wards and aeroplanes,
we place our unresolved struggles into
the open hands of darkness,
to be held softly, tenderly,
until tomorrow comes.

7:3

Waking

In the liminal space between being fast asleep and being fully awake lies a basketful of possibilities. Sometimes, the birthing of a new idea seems to have arrived unbidden yet has a freedom before the physical world begins its demands. Sometimes the reconfiguring of dreams and nightmares places the aspirations and terrors in a different place, brings amazement at the convoluted complexity of the imagination. Sometimes, as night recedes, there is anticipation or dread returning for the day ahead. In this betwixt and between place, that is neither sleeping nor being awake, we ask for enough time to smile, to bolster our courage, to be peaceful enough for whatever struggles or adventures or routines lie ahead.

Walking

How much resolve is needed
to ease the bolted doors?
How much grief unheeded
before the killings cease?
How much blood and treasure
poured out to settle scores
between the pacts and anguish
could we measure space for peace?

Seeing

Between these two possibilities—that you are winning and that you have no chance of winning—there is a place for truce or pact, treaty or surrender. Into this space step two adversaries, honour and common sense. The first says that we should always defend what we believe is sacrosanct; the latter finds pragmatic solutions at the expense of justice or the rights of the vulnerable. To stand looking in both directions at the same time, to hold the vistas of both defeat and triumph but achieve neither, to disarm the pride of individuals or nations, is both a supremely powerful and a supremely powerless place. Maybe peace is a passive as well as an active verb, a way in which to stand between contradicting powers and say, "There could be another way."

Acting

The Arms Fair is to be held again in London. Some will protest, some will pray, some will write articles, some will draw the attention of the media, but the weapons will be sold and the human rights of many will continue to be violated. How do we make sense of this madness? The excuse is always defence, that if we are undefended then we will be annihilated, but in our very defensiveness we are perpetual aggressors. What a bizarre rhetoric this is, that by buying weapons we will be safer!

Creating

Ploughing dark furrows,
painting earth's sorrows,
planting a tree.
Striding green landscapes,
dancing word rhythms,
sketching rough sea.
Weaving loose tatters,
sculpting love poems,
shaping a bowl.
Striding etched coastlines,
spinning grey lambswool,
freeing the soul.

Becoming

Working in interreligious dialogue can be challenging at times: there are all the cultural and societal and faith assumptions to negotiate. It can be even more challenging if a person lives within a completely different social and cultural mix. This was so for Alex who had moved to a predominately Muslim British city and whose neighbours spoke very little English. He found that he spent the first year of the experience imagining he was on a foreign tour, then confronting himself as a minority in his own country. There were times of resentment, of inner racism, of loneliness and sometimes anger. He experienced all the feelings of isolation that many immigrants recount, and yet this was *his* country, or so he had told himself. Then one day he was asked to pop around to his Muslim neighbours where an uncle of the extended family had just died. He sat on a large leather sofa, eating snacks and feeling completely out of his depth. When he started to take his leave, "Please pray with us," the family requested. Stifling an inner panic as to how a Christian should pray in a Muslim household without anyone taking offence, he closed his eyes and prayed from the heart. He discovered in that moment that love can pray in any language.

Reflecting

- Is there ever any justification for selling Arms?
- When is "peace" a passive rather than an active word?
- Where are the imaginative spaces for alternative creativity?

Resting

Everything looks different
from the place you end up.
In retrospect
much is forgiven
by the kindness of time.
In the heft and heave
of the trivia of everyday life,
trauma, shock,
dislocations of war,
the still point is
the unfathomable depth
of one's own tenacious spirit.
Between joy and melancholy,
is a balcony for watching the stars,
for gazing, for reverie,
for cleansing the tortures of memory,
for standing.

Blessing

Dreams not terrors,
rest not fear,
peace not warfare,
love draw near.

7:4

Waking

There are those who open their eyes but see no light; their eyesight is impaired or maybe they can see only darkness through mental ill health. Either way the morning is still dark. There are those who wake to foreboding, because there is the sound of gunfire outside or they have remembered that their worst dreams have become reality.

There are those who open their eyes and see no light, there are those that wake to fear. We remember these people as we begin this day.

Walking

There is a myth that everything in the city is harsh and aggressive and disruptive, whilst everything in the countryside is gentle and passive and tranquil; neither of these things are true. We tend to think that we can "escape to the country", and yet the rural communities have some of the highest numbers of suicides. We tend to think that all that is bad is related to concrete and steel, whilst all that is restorative is about trees and birds and flowers, yet cities offer art and music and design in magnificent ways. Stereotypes, binaries: they are usually unhelpful because they "other", and once we "other", we are closer to seeing those different from ourselves as enemies.

Seeing

The academic and the filmmaker both ask this question: "What is your observer position?" For the researcher, the position of the observer is critical to their methodology, the need to ascertain how much they are detached and how much they are involved in the data they are gathering. For the filmmaker, the question is about where the audience is positioned; are they viewing events through the eyes of the protagonists or from a distant, objective place? This question resonates with ordinary lives too. Are we observers of reality from afar or are we participants that are absorbed by and into the events that are taking place? Acknowledging our observer or participant position is key in any sort of mediation or attempt at reconciliation. None of us are totally neutral; some of us do not feel the passion in the same way as others whose more intimate involvement will affect the way everything appears to them.

Acting

Currently everyone around us appears to be in crisis. This might be because their marriages are falling apart, or that they have new loves, or that they have critical health issues, or they are stressed and anxious about work, home or family. This seems true also of the headlines. We are presented each day with crisis and angst; everything seems precarious or tumultuous or precipitous. Crisis is exhausting and troubling but ultimately numbing; we turn off from it and try to ignore it; we simply want to live our daily lives in the presence of actual events. I wonder how, as peacemakers, we can live within the outer narrative of crisis whilst still maintaining an everyday perspective on what is real and what is possible.

Creating

He was just two years old and playing with the logs in the front garden. He was pulling them from the stack where they were stored in anticipation of the winter fires. He pulled one from the top of the pile which was uneven in shape with the end of three branches poking out at various angles. He declared that it was a triceratops; he no longer had just sticks but a stash of dinosaurs! Imagination grows with us as we interpret the world around us, we no longer see just sticks but give objects meaning, character, personality, possibility. As we imagine the world differently, as we see the potential in inanimate objects, as we ponder the wider possibilities of creation, so too we are able to become creative, conceive of making something new.

Becoming

So many delusions, secrets,
trysts closeted,
clever double-crosses,
discrete illicit loves,
supposed proficiency.
So much rawness, covered,
relying on distraction,
lack of care masked as efficiency,
lies, shadow-blankets,
elusive truth.
Such contrived conceit,
unruly deeds, corrupt bosses.
So many captured, silenced,
greed enraptured,
trapped, incomplete.
So many memories unrecovered,
aspirations fractured,
un-replete, complicit,
in the deceit of
the illusion of sufficiency.

Reflecting

- When have we been particularly aware of our "observer position"?
- How might we begin to imagine something new?
- Could we rethink our view of the urban environment to find beauty?

Resting

We pray that the dead will "rest in peace", but what do we mean? Are we asking that their earthly struggles will be resolved? No, clearly these conflicts will outlive them and someone else will be taking up the mantle. Are we asking that they will somehow be in a place without pain, turbulence and struggle? Certainly, but why are we praying this? Do we really think that pain and struggle could continue after death, are we still pleading with the Almighty? Are we actually saying that we hope they are not caused or causing trouble any more so that we can get on better without them, knowing we are forgiven? Is it true that we find no rest until we rest in God, and is this simply something afforded to us after death? Can we find rest and peace this side of dying? Answers on a postcard appreciated!

Blessing

Bless this damaged day
with healing,
this discordant day
with resolution,
this troublesome day,
with peace.

8:1

Waking

If I wake this day with remembered conflict,
unfinished business,
unresolved hurts,
I will brush the dust from the feet of yesterday
stride into a new potential
for healing, trust and hope.

Walking

My friend asked me why the Church found relationships so difficult. It's hard to answer without further questions. Maybe because we have framed the holy family as perfect, maybe because we are conflicted about our relationship with the poor, maybe because we have no clear instructions as to how relationships should happen. Or it could be because the biblical narrative is about a turbulent, stormy, messed-up yet faithful relationship with God. Life is messed up, and so it's maybe not so perplexing that the Church has found relationships difficult, because humanity has always found relationships difficult.

Seeing

A sailor, looking out at the horizon from the deck of a super-tanker, might see reflections on the horizon of other ships, some larger than life, others upside down. These are mirages that float a long way away, suggesting spectres of other realms, other lives, other dimensions. These images could play havoc with the imagination of those already surrounded by the sea, calling to mind ghosts and other worlds. Fear and wonder combine in the apparitions refracted by light, asking questions of their humanity and their vulnerability on the edge of the ocean.

Acting

The internet doubles the speed of gossip. The immediate sharing of ideas and news can clutter the mind and the virtual airways with opinions. It might seem to be white noise but at times this incessant chatter can become malignant, infecting the thinking and prejudices of millions who look to this stream to inform their own opinions. In this way, lives, families, confidence, trust can be destroyed in an instant. How to act peaceably? Is it to challenge, is it to ignore, is it to converse? Who knows?

Creating

Walking down the steps in the grey, dew-laden morning, I see the finest of silver threads spanning the holly tree and the hawthorn bush just before the gate. The dog ducks under it easily; for me there is the need to double over and slide downwards so I do not break the spider's nocturnal activity. I wonder at the remarkable antics of the night, in which the tiny creature has launched itself over the footpath to land on the other side, and I consider its daring creativity. Then I ponder the spider's immense tenacity and courage, and how much we have feared it and endeavoured to brush it away.

Becoming

There is this assumed great divide between those who are considered to be academic and those whose gifts are creative or practical. Maybe this divide is the coat-tail of the British class system that lingers in the psyche of a nation that defines itself by rank. There are those that consider academics snobs and wasters by virtue of their perceived absorption in the ethereal or the imaginative. There are those that consider creatives or practical people "airy fairy" or condescendingly "good with their hands". This divide is reinforced by economic differentials and discrepancies in opportunities. Peace within the mores of social structures are hard to notice, let alone challenge, but as soon as we have defined another within a category of our own making, we are not peacemakers.

Reflecting

Let the peace of Christ rule in your hearts, since as **members of one body** you were called to peace. And be thankful.

The Colossians reading reminds us that we are members of one body, one community and that if we are "to peace", then we cannot do it alone.

- Who have we, deliberately or unwittingly, defined as less than ourselves?
- Whose daring courage scares us?
- What could we do to reduce harmful internet gossip?

Resting

In the community of the night,
we lie in solidarity with those who
this day have sought to heal rifts or mend wounds.
May I know, and may they know, that this night
we are a community,
a community of struggle, a community of possibilities.

Blessing

There are nights of sorrows,
and nights of regret,
there are nights of no return
and nights of earth's darkest shadows.
From all these nights somehow birth
tomorrow's peace,
in whatever ways are yet possible.

8:2

Waking

We pray this will not be a day of wrangling,
of niggles or grumpiness,
rather a day of wriggling free of expectations,
smiling at adversaries,
unnerving the expectations of conflict.
We pray that today will contradict
the dull drudgery of apathy,
or the insidious drip feed of unrest,
that there will be spaciousness, grace and gratitude
in the attitudes we both portray and encounter.

Walking

He was having a conversation with a musician who was explaining the spaces between notes, the tiny variations in sound that were not defined or resolved by the keyboard, which were hardly perceptible to the human ear. This conversation later put him in mind of a Terry Pratchett novel in which there was a part of the spectrum stretching beyond sight that included other colours that nobody could see and yet were present.

He began to muse about these gaps between things and these colours and those imperceptible sounds, and he began to realize that the angst and stress that he was feeling needed this sort of perspective, the ability to see the infinite spaces between the things that were presenting themselves as normal, the vast array of possibility beyond the spectrum of life, beyond the finite vista he thought he had understood.

Seeing

We only truly see ourselves when we see others; we only really understand others when we are acquainted with the contours of our own landscape. If we are truly to see each other, we need to view the maps of our identities, scan the longitude, the altitude, the latitude, and valleys of our personal geographies. We can only understand each other if we stand on a geo-political atlas, note the refugee journeys of migration, empire, emigration, immigration, our own refugee status, our intersecting journeys, our shared longings for a homeland. To see all this is to know the meaning of belonging, alienation, the dispossession and struggles for power within which we are all complicit and yet equally human.

Acting

Unmask this world to me,
unshoe the unheard clogs of drudgery,
unleash the ties of toil, or torment,
let me see where blue horizons lie
where mirage holds humanity,
oil and water muddle into peacock-feather blue,
meld together to reflect the
iridescent sky.
Take off this cloak of reason, let me see
the hues of shine that puddle
in the tears I speak,
in the words I cry.

Creating

In Alice Springs, there is not a lot of compost, or rain or duration
to any season. A downpour comes rarely. The riverbed is normally
dry, the flowers wait more than a year, hunkering down in the
parched earth before they dare to scent water and bloom. Out
back, somewhere out there, in a distant community away from the
city, there are the indigenous people who understand the lands and
the seasons and the creatures that find shade under the rocks and
in the shadow of verandas, waiting for their moment to emerge.
They hold stories and understanding of the sacred and earthed,
and they also remember the violent clearance of their people from
their sacred lands to make way for what others called civilization
or progress. Their children remain displaced, skirting the edges
of the cities, laden with alcohol or confusion. History has parched
their land; it is not only the rain that is missing: it is justice too.

Becoming

Today has been spent scraping wallpaper off a bedroom wall. The top layer was a child's pink Disney cartoon, then glittery paper, and under that was a layer of paint, then some ochre 1970s mustard-coloured paper, and then lining paper, and then finally, on the bare plaster, the initials of some children who had been allowed to scrawl on the distemper before the wallpaper was put up.

So many layers, like the Russian doll of our lives, childhood, teenage rebellion, the painting over of things. All those layers lying curled up on the floor, mixed and muddled.

Reflecting

- How could we understand the trauma of displacement and begin to make amends?
- Do we only truly know ourselves in relationship with others?
- Where are the gaps between things?

Resting

As the day draws to a close,
I bring to mind all those
whom I have met or remembered,
whose names I have forgotten
or whose stories I only half heard.
In the tiredness of this twilight,
I ask for forgiveness
for my lack of attention and focus.
As I ask for peace to surround me,
I ask also for forgotten stories to be redeemed
by greater love than mine.

Blessing

As evening turns russet to auburn,
the dull curtains of dusk
are ruptured
by fissures of light,
so, send peace to the world,
crack open dark places
with surprising rays of hope.

8:3

Waking

Breakfast should not be complicated: it should be a simple act, a sacramental pause before the breaking open of the day. But in community it becomes complicated; there are others to negotiate, queues to join with cups, toast to wait for, trays to clear. Finding the sacrament of this community requires fortitude, patience, good humour, coffee!

Walking

I watch the mother tugging the child's arm as they make their way towards school. I recall how early the mornings used to start when ours were that age. However organized we had felt the night before, there were always missing shoes, forgotten homework, tooth brushing to nag about. And in the school yard, a turning on the heels with a deep breath, trying to relinquish worry, trying to feel a good enough parent. Peace was not a word we used much in those days, except to describe the absence of the tsunami of children.

Seeing

It has become such a challenge to confront our own racism, to notice our privilege, to acknowledge our own complicity in the slavery of others. There is so much work to be done, both in our communities and in our souls! It is hard to know where to begin, not to despair, how to reform our assumptions, our expectations. Yet how can there be peace in our communities unless those of us with power, even a power we never knew we had, can somehow use it to empower others, to make equality not just our ideal but our everyday intention and practice? To say that we are sorry is not enough, our contrition must become our reformation.

Acting

The pastors had come crowded into cars, on bicycles, on motorbikes or on foot. They had stayed overnight, sleeping in one room on low beds, head to foot, their dusty bare feet protruding from under colourful blankets. This was a clergy training week in Pakistan. They cooked outside, ate sitting around trees on the bare earth around the cathedral. Their faces had the calligraphy of struggle, fear and yes, laughter. They had come from the rural communities or other parts of the city and they lived as a Christian minority amongst many who were hostile to them, who often refused to use the same cups as they did, limited their access to water or education. Yet in the evening they sang their hymns and listened to the scriptures, prayed for their communities, shared their stories. As the sun went down, so they also hunkered down in their simple quarters, taking time out to be together and consider how to live peaceably enough in their place.

Creating

He said he loved teaching and plants. He said in both occupations his greatest delight was to nurture the ones that were straggling and give them just the right amount of water, to make sure they were neither drenched nor parched. He said that, mysteriously, he had the ability to make things flourish; this was not bragging, just how it seemed to be for him. On her first day of teaching, he brought her a pot plant with the proviso that if it looked as if it was struggling for love or water, at any time at all, she should seek him out.

Becoming

Peace is Christ's farewell gift. It is more than peace of mind or the tranquillity of a good conscience; it is the participation in God's own life. It is the remembering of this holy broken body in bread and wine; it is a call to live the Eucharist in the humdrum ordinariness of life. To participate in this peace is to participate in struggle, not alone but rather within the community of other odd bods that consider they are part of the ramshackle community of faith. The kingdom of God is lived out in this way, in this cracked vessel of humanity that longs for redemption, for themselves and for the whole of creation. This is always a work in progress; it is always our work.

Reflecting

- How could we become more aware of inequalities of power?

- Where do we spend good time in relationship with others?
- What can we do differently to enable others to flourish?

Resting

The harvest moon takes her turn to illuminate the sky,
just as the North Star and the Great
    Bear have taken their watch
in due season,
the waxing gibbous and the waning crescent have
patrolled their orbits,
hosted their own shadows,
turned their faces
to the setting and the rising of the sun.
So it is, we humans, dust of stars,
dreaming of other things,
take our turn and patrol our patch
until, like the heavens above,
we turn our faces to the night sky.

Blessing

Bless this eternity
this uncertainty,
this complexity.
Bless with peace
this wondrous, mighty,
fragile mystery.

8:4

Waking

Shake bitterness from our heads,
brush regret from our feet,
wash assumptions from our eyes.
Adorn this day with kindness,
clothe this day with mercy,
dress this day with peace.

Walking

Toxic narratives are easy to spot once they have become
ideologies, less easy to notice as they worm their way into the
everyday discourse of fear. We might be horrified by what we
perceive to be the hatred of the dictator or the terrorist, but not
notice the sly infiltration that happens each day in the press
article or social media post. The vocabulary of hatred comes
one word at a time, one nagging doubt at a time, one convincing
uncertainty at a time, until there is a whole dictionary justifying
its own definitions. Justice and peace must always punctuate
opinions with a question mark not a full stop, offer a counter-
narrative to the rhetoric of warfare, resolutely deconstruct the
language of fear.

Seeing

Inside the metal box, which itself was inside a bunker in the middle of an airfield, two military personnel were watching a screen on which a man was hiding under a bush. The man was in the Middle East; the metal box was in Britain. The means of observation was a drone which hovered above the bush and was controlled remotely by the two observers. They had been watching the man all morning, and shortly they were going to change shift and let two others take over the surveillance. These two officers needed to get changed and go to collect their kids from school. The man under the bush was not going to do that.

Acting

Maybe our greatest sin is not that we do the wrong thing but rather that we do nothing at all. This could be through apathy, but most likely it is because we see the whole mess of things and believe that nothing can be done. Cheery people encourage us to do one small thing, but in our hearts we know that it is pointless: the principalities and powers are too pervasive, the economic drivers too compelling, the arguments for defence too logical to resist. We despair; we hunker down; we try to be positive. How can we move out of this numbness, to mobilize in a meaningful way? How could we be more peaceful together than alone?

Creating

The bread was rising in the heat of the sun. "We must listen to what the bread is telling us," one woman said, and the others nodded as they rested themselves against the wall or perched their wide bodies on plastic chairs, rubbing their floury hands into their laps. The township had been decimated by AIDS; the grannies were raising the children alone; there was not enough food for everyone. The children would come after school and wait for the bread and hold out their plastic containers for the stew that was bubbling over the charcoal fire. Some had no container; they simply held out their hands. "We must listen to what the bread is telling us," she said.

Becoming

Take, eat,
let this crumbling,
wafer-thin morsel of grace
break your solitude.
Sip this bitter wine,
a chalice tipped
onto parched lips of despair.
You are as broken and bloodied
as this meagre feast,
as hungry as you were before,
yet in this simple company,
the word takes flesh.

Reflecting

- How is the word becoming flesh amongst us?
- Where has despair paralysed our ability to change?
- In the face of remote warfare, what is our peaceful response?

Resting

He sat down at the table under the bamboo-leaf roof. The sun that had seared the day was now retreating, and a light breeze ruffled the wisp of white hair that fell across his forehead. He drank beer and spoke about the puppets. They were a tradition of the border tribes, these roughly carved marionettes that danced on long strings, whose limbs dangled jauntily and danced cross-legged on the brightly coloured carpet. The puppets, he explained, helped children to tell their stories, helped them laugh, took away the nightmares of the trauma through which they had lived. Seven years old, and your village was burned, your mother carried you away into the mountains, you were hungry and afraid, the darkness was all terror. The puppets knew all this, their wooden arms made friendlier shadows, they made you laugh and play like children again.

Blessing

Hold our grief and gratitude,
all hurts and hazards,
all friends and frenzies,
all dreams and dreads.
Hold us, each and all
rest us each and all,
shade us each and all,
bless us each and all.

9:1

Waking

Falling awake
we descend
above sleep.
Surfacing below,
tangled dreams
we plummet upwards,
towards daylight.

Walking

So much of life is transitory, transitional, temporary. The spiritual life is often defined as the journey, pilgrimage a metaphor for the eternal quest. Even when we are going slowly, we are "walking with God" towards some spiritual destination. And all this language of movement, of eschatology, of redemption and salvation is always pointing us forwards, towards some end point that is at best aspirational and at worst impossible. Our homecoming is always beyond us, just out of reach, out of sight, over the horizon. Yet peace is not, should not, be in such a category. Whilst peace is elusive it is also a place to dwell; to be at peace is to be at home in the present moment. Peace is our abode, our shelter, our grounding, our dwelling place.

So that this shalom, this salaam, this namaste becomes the everyday greeting between humans, between their longings, between their friendships, between their faiths, between their connections to the divine.

Seeing

Show us this most excellent way—
sparks of glory in the ordinary,
glimmers of hope in the melancholy,
glints of prayer in the drudgery,
surprise of change in the mystery.
Show us this most excellent way.

Acting

We are all activists now. We are all people that can flip the script, hurl question marks at the folly of the world. We are an event, not a text. We are an action, not a position. We are the music, the march, the solidarity, the change. We are the cantilever span across the absurdly divided banks of injustice, inequality and oppression. Whilst we have breath, whilst we have anger, whilst we have faith, whilst we have passion, we are all activists.

Creating

He was writing a story. He had an initial idea for a plot, but he did not yet know how it would unfold. As he wrote he found the story talking back to him; he began to envisage the people he had created, the bars and hotels they inhabited, the wild open plains of a land he had never visited. He began to love the story and found in a strange way that it was writing him. Formerly he had found the tyranny of a blank page intimidating but now he deliberately left the day's writing halfway through a line so that all night he could anticipate the next word. He and the story became so closely joined that he ached for her friendship and, although he wanted to get to a conclusion, at the same time he didn't want her exquisite company to become another's property. The passion between him and the story was all embracing, as he gave the story life, so the story changed him too: he became both the storyteller and the words.

Becoming

The teaching session was about the human lifecycle and how to reflect on it theologically. There was some set reading, drawing on sociology and psychological research; there were insights into the stages of faith and some delving into biblical texts. The students were attentive and took notes; they absorbed the theories and began to plan their essays. But, whilst the tutor hoped they would be able to navigate their way through all these books and that she would be able to give them a good grade for their assignment, secretly she hoped that they would say "Bunkum!" That they would shrug their shoulders at the theory and laugh out loud at the idea that somehow life was linear.

That they would see the intersectionality of it all, the search for gender identity, the chaos of mental ill health, the impact of ethnicity and racism, the losses that were beyond logic. That they would be able to see the beauty of this eternally painful life and discover the mysterious laughter and torment at the heart of divine wisdom.

Reflecting

> Let the peace of Christ rule *in your hearts*, since as members of one body you were called to peace. And be thankful.

If peace is to rule in our hearts, then it needs to become a daily pattern:

- How could we begin to find peace in small things?
- If peace is a doing word, are we all activists?
- When is the concept of faith being a journey unhelpful for us?

Resting

Regimes fold and ideologies fall,
strategies falter and certainties fade,
icons are reduced to celebrities,
grand visions to daily chores.
The disillusion of the narrative of peace
turns sagas to short stories,
phrases into hollow words.
In the hymnody of the night
we turn to you,
origin of good,
asking that you will give us scale,
that tragedy will not be reduced to column inches,
that minutiae will not escalate
into the headlines of war.

Blessing

In the summit meetings,
in the staff meetings,
in the church meetings,
in the family meetings,
help us to
reach out in peaceful blessing
across the table that divides us,
meeting each other's needs,
being each other's hope.

9:2

Waking

From all that deceives, deliver us.
From all that shames, release us.
From all that diminishes, free us.
Let this day have forbearance.
Let this day have patience.
Let this day have spontaneity.
Towards understanding, lead us.
Towards reconciliation, prompt us.
Towards peace, invigorate us.

Walking

It seems that advocates for war are often more eloquent than the protagonists of peace. Treachery, grievance, wrath: they each provoke a response to violence. It often appears that it is harder for the peacemakers to get their voices heard than it is for the troublemakers, that anger screams louder than reconciliation. Similarly, we shout more loudly about one individual murder than a genocide; we are more concerned about one neighbourhood's injustice than the violent vanquishing of whole nations. Warfare brings clouds, storms, thunder, whereas peace must offer a climate of integrity, arbitration and diplomacy. The olive tree grows slowly, but the rage of fire can soon destroy it.

Seeing

He could remember when they changed from imperial to metric measurement. He had been in school to run out in the lunch hour to try to buy sweets for pence p not pence d. It was as if the whole world had been recalibrated, the worth of things had been reconfigured, the value had changed dimension into quantities they no longer understood. That was many years ago and now it all seems normal, hardly anyone remembers pence d. If we are to live by a rule of peace, how can we do that in relation to the old rule of warfare, how can we measure things differently, how can we recalibrate our learned, habitual experiences by the numeracy of peace?

Acting

They had enjoyed a holiday in Alice Springs, visiting Uluru and seeing the sacred cave drawing. On their way to "the red centre" of Australia, they had been hearing the stories of the early white migrants who had founded cattle ranches there. They visited a village in the wilderness, amongst the Ghost Gums and the wind, stepping around the burned-out car and visiting the community centre where they had hoped maybe they could buy an "aboriginal painting" for their living room. It would be added to the stories they could tell their friends about their travels. But they were not rich, and the cost of an original painting was beyond them.

On another day in Alice, they visited the old gaol, where years before indigenous people had been held in captivity, whilst their lands were reapportioned by the white people, where those ancient custodians of the land had been robbed and spat at and degraded. In the corner of the gift shop was a simple rolled up piece of canvas, where dots of rudimentary colour and kangaroo footprints had been formed into a pattern. The painting was not "fine art"; on the contrary it was very cheap—after all it had been made by a present-day prisoner. They bought it anyway, and later, with some pieces of dried Ghost Gum bark, they framed it. This simple canvas now told a different and salutary story, one in which they were no longer innocent tourists unable to ignore their colonial history, a history by which they were also convicted.

Creating

These ragged sacrifices to fear,
quarrels that unravel sense,
arguments that unpick reason,
they wear forbearance thin,
these unyielding knots of war.
Give me at least a sewing needle
to begin amending,
a remnant of light to
join the tattered threads
within embattled arguments.
Assist me in attending
to the frayed tempers,
the snags and tangled ends
of this world-worn holy garment.

Becoming

Maybe one of the biggest threats to reconciliation is litigation. It seems that people would often be prepared to acknowledge their faults and say sorry if it wasn't that to do so would make them liable, so they dare not. The fear of being convicted or of being in the headlines, or of being disenfranchised from a place of belonging, means that those of us who are mistaken in some error or other, have no space to repent. Why is it that the press and the law have so much control over us that there is little room for the grace to say sorry?

Reflecting

- When have we not repented of a mistake for fear of not being forgiven?
- Where in our shared history do we carry responsibility for disenfranchising indigenous communities?
- How could we make amends?

Resting

We ask that tonight we will find the grace to
    take responsibility for our mistakes,
the wisdom not to carry what is not ours to bear,
the gravitas to be grounded at the fulcrum of justice,
the desire to welcome tomorrow as if it
    were our first and last day.
The world is turbulent enough and many
    suffer for harsh reasons,

we adhere to the surface, conscious of
    our own remiss and remorse,
turning to the wise one who dwells within us
and the sage that dwells beyond us.
We come contrite and determined
to live within a better way
resolving, over and over,
to walk a peaceful path.

Blessing

Bless this night
the little ones,
the troubled ones,
the lost ones,
the lonely ones,
for in them Jesus has seen
the holy ones,
the blessed ones.

9:3

Waking

It was the 1980s, and their university accommodation was small and cramped. They shared a bedroom and there were woodlice behind the woodchip wallpaper. In the morning, her roommate used to ask, "Are you woken?", and it seemed to her rather quaint and northern and a long way from home. Now, nearly fifty years later, society asks, "Are you woke?" and the word has trans-morphed into another sort of awareness. The question is not about opening one's eyes to another morning in damp digs and a day in the college lab, but rather to the wide vista of life's glorious diversity and cultural heritage, and also to the day's inherited discrimination and bias. Back then, it was the woodlice that worked away at the surrounding fabric, now it is the inherited awakening to colonialism, racism and the legacy of capitalism that gnaw away at our complacency.

Walking

There are ways of discerning justice, maximizing welfare, freedom of choice, the cultivation of virtue. Arguments go to and fro; we balance one person's justice against another's, one country's against an opponent's. Inevitably there is conflict, and this conflict is not necessarily bad; it just needs space to find a place for dialogue, for negotiation, for reconciliation, for humanizing the issues. Justice is a contested language: it depends on the lens you have, the cultural inheritance you inhabit, the economic framework you assume. Justice and peace may walk the same pathway, but they do not necessarily have the same destination.

Seeing

In the quick blink,
eyelids close their
shutters on truth.
In flash of gun
a child's breath
is spent.
In splitting a second,
or atom
the half-life
burns the heart from the tree, the city,
the old lady gathering her washing,
the market, the family wedding,
the meal.
In the impact of a moment
worlds are shattered,
peace splinters.

Acting

When you look at me, do you see the image of God? Do you see someone that is as loved as you know yourself to be loved, or do you, in the split second between seeing me and passing some cultured pleasantry, think to yourself for just a moment, this person is black or strange or smelly or old or rough? Just for that fraction before your outer self gets your inner self to conform, do you think that I am less than you, not quite whom God intended? Be honest now, because if you do, and you can remember that you do, then that is at least a start.

Creating

Today the winners of the Nobel Peace Prize, despite their modesty, raise a glass to their unexpected acclaim. Even though we do not know their names, even though their work is unknown to us, they are revered, honoured, held in the highest regard.

Meanwhile, in an olive grove a solitary farmer on a parched hillside, unheralded, plants a new tree.

Becoming

It is no coincidence that the words "grief" and "grievance" share the same root. Grief takes its varied pathways, through disbelief, anger, sadness and remorse, not necessarily in that order and certainly not in a straight line. Ultimately, the bereft find a way of functioning around the loss they continue to feel; there is no "getting over it", rather a way of absorbing absence into everyday living. Is it possible then, if this grief remains raw, unaccommodated or buried, it will surface in grievance? Is it true that when we experience what appears to be irrational anger from another the root of this could lie within an unresolved experience of loss? Is it possible that as a nation who claimed we were victorious in the Second World War, our grief morphed into "putting it all behind us" and was never properly aired? After all, collective grief is hard to express. Could this explain (but not excuse) some of the resentment that simmers in our society and bubbles up in nationalism, selfish capitalism and grievances?

Reflecting

- Whom do we honour and why?
- Are grief and grievance related?
- What should we be free from, what should we be free for?

Resting

There is a stone on the A83 in Scotland which was originally placed there by soldiers who completed the military road in 1753. The stone is inscribed with the words, "Rest and be Thankful". Set in spectacular but treacherous landscape, with the vista of Ben Arthur scratching the scuttering clouds, the stone offers a place for reverie beneath the brooding clouds and dark history that overshadow Glen Coe.

As we conclude this day, we sit in similar surroundings. The world is not at peace, and the clatter of warfare echoes between the mountains; the storm clouds gather between nations; others flee violence or traumatic memories. Nevertheless, maybe we, who lead comfortable enough lives, could sit a while, absorbed by the exquisite beauty of the natural world, or observing closely the face of someone we love. Maybe such a pause on the journey, like those soldiers who placed the stone in such a hostile landscape, could enable us to "rest and be thankful" before we resolve again to continue constructing a new highway.

Blessing

Bundle up this day
into your carpet bag of grace,
sling it lovingly
over your shoulder,
as an incomplete project,
your unfinished work of art.

9:4

Waking

Awaken in us
a spirit of righteousness,
a thirst for justice,
an attitude of humility.
Awaken in us the strength
to relinquish violence,
and actively resist oppression.
Awaken us to exploration
of peaceful means,
of protest and resistance.

Walking

How often has peace been an excuse for war? The conviction that this one act of violence, this blunderbuss, this barrage balloon, this ballistic missile, this atomic bomb, will somehow finish everything off so that after this one last act of extreme violence then peace will prevail. We are artisans of illusion, deluded by our own flawed opinions, unwilling to settle for an incomplete peace, convinced that one last battle will resolve the issues and bring something lasting. We ponder all this from our own sense of power, as if we can control destiny; we take it upon ourselves to be the defenders of righteousness according to our Western economic and political blueprints. We look for justice and mercy but forget that we are also called to walk humbly with our God.

Seeing

Our longing for peace needs to come from the overwhelming sense of the earth's beauty, the intricacy and balance of the environment, the mystery of life. Everything else should come from this, economic equity, pursuit of justice, arbitration not obliteration. For people of faith, it begins with the relationship of the Creator with creation, a theology that insists that the earth is good and that all humankind is equally made in the image of love. To see the world as beautiful is to ache for it, to see the tender balance of things and the foolishness of fighting each other. It is to believe that we need to quell our territorial and economic greed in order to save this extraordinary, holy thing called life. It is vocational and transformative and divinely essential that we pattern our lives to this way of peace.

Acting

It is curious to me, how somebody that really doesn't like shopping and certainly only goes for things that she needs, ends up with so much "stuff"! I like to blame the "buy one get one free" ads or the free unwanted gifts that come along with legitimate purchases, but really it is quite clear that I am prone to buy much more than I need. It's not just depressing, these endless trips to the tip or the recycling bin, it's wrong. Why am

I surrounded by things that clutter my house and make me feel hemmed in by materialism? And why am I so unable to behave in ways that preserve the environment and prevent climate change? Trying to live simply, simply isn't simple!

Creating

His footwork was surprisingly nimble, his suit shabby and his fine leather shoes had a sole flip-flopping as he danced. She held him within this situation they could not have contemplated, that had left their middle-class life as tattered as their clothes. Her smile had been painted on carelessly with cheap but bright lipstick, and although his shirt had no collar, he wore a tie. They offered to show us how to tango, in that homeless hostel in Buenos Aires that was now their home. We applauded their courage and their resilience but we could not comprehend their pain, how the political and economic crash had so deeply impacted their lives, status and identity. They danced oblivious for a moment to their predicament. Afterwards we knew we had witnessed the drama of a nation in the pattern of their steps.

Becoming

Between these two possibilities:
that you are winning,
that you have no chance of winning,
a sparrow falls.
This dead thing dropping on the mossy earth
means nothing,
counts for everything,
says, there is no winning for either party
just life and death,
a slender branch between them,
always the possibility of falling.

Reflecting

- How can our desire for things be modified to protect the environment?
- Can we resist territorial greed peacefully?
- Is peace used as an excuse for war?

Resting

The sabbatical of the night draws us once again into the world of dreams. It says, enough of this day for now and it is time to let go. Just as we heard that God rested on the seventh day to stand back from the labour of creation, we stand aside from the disappointment of betrayal, from the fall-out of the human story. The world is beautiful and fragile and so are we, the earth is finite and generous and so are we, the earth is luxuriant and damaged, and so are we. We enter the sabbatical of the night to rest, whilst the glorious globe turns, while light moves from one hemisphere to the next. We are but mortal, fallible, gullible and thwarted, but we trust in the resurrection of the new day the other side of this darkness.

Blessing

As the lamppost watches over the street,
the tower block keeps vigil over the playground's swings,
the silent trees canopy the park,
transactions of the night subvert the darkness,
so may we offer this damaged and glorious
    day into your keeping,
resetting the table,
in anticipation of tomorrow's breakfast.

10:1

Waking

Pray your vision into me this day,
pray through me, without me and within me.
Let me embody your love, inside and out.
Give me a centre of loving melancholy,
the face of insistent hope.
Incarnate God, born into suffering,
challenged by forces beyond your control,
bring me to the heart of Jesus,
bring me to the centre of life,
of this life, of all life.

Walking

The imperative for peace seems to be most pressing in times of war, and in times of relative peace it is not promoted positively. It seems we are always caught out by violence when it erupts from the simmering of low-level discontent. Racism, injustice, inequality, prejudice, they are all so "normal" that we, who are so often cushioned from poverty and discrimination, are surprised and indignant when tempers come to the boil. Positive peacemaking means attention to this inequality in times that seem tranquil, a constant push towards equality, listening and deliberate relinquishing of power when we are off our guard.

Seeing

Fell the trees of resentment
that have rooted in our wounds,
clear this bitter ground,
uproot our vengeful thoughts,
and in this clearing,
pitch tents of meeting.
Sow new stories
in the freshly turned
tilth of forgiveness.

Acting

She was not even five feet tall and was eighty-six years old. She said that she would not sit with any one group after morning worship but that she would "mingle". And so it was that the church that told everybody outside that it was friendly but ignored newcomers began to be changed. It wasn't obvious what she was up to as she chatted to the toddlers in the corner or the old chap with his wheelchair parked at the edge of the room, as she waved at the shy couple who had dared to come for the first time or the taxi driver waiting to collect the confused old lady. She was just "mingling" and transforming a community in the process.

Creating

We are creation's possible people,
ligaments holding together,
flexed and perplexed,
speaking our puzzlements,
flawed, lavish, broken,
flailing around in thickets of uncertainty, yet
wrapped in grace,
clutching at the hem of love.

Becoming

He would never describe himself as anything other than an ordinary bloke. He'd had a few relationships, even been married once, worked at various satisfactory, if unfulfilling, jobs, moved around a bit but tried to keep in touch with a handful of friends. Then, when one of these friends was in trouble and came over late one night and asked for somewhere to stay, after only a moment's hesitation he made up the sofa bed. He never asked for how long; he never wanted an explanation; he never probed into the circumstances of this crisis. He simply said, "Yes, here's a bed" and left it at that.

Reflecting

Let the peace of Christ rule in your hearts, since as members of *one body* you were called to peace. And be thankful.

In this reading we are reminded that peace and creativity go hand in hand. Creativity is not simply the act of making something, but rather the interaction between humans and the earth that draws us into deeper relationship with the divine.

- When did an "ordinary" person make an extraordinary difference in our lives?
- How can we be positive peacemakers in peaceful times?
- Who has shown us what hospitality means?

Resting

Enough of this day's questions,
the transgressive imagination
scaling the stone walls of certainty.
Enough of the lies and banter, a newscaster's take on reality.
Enough of all the posturing and preening,
enough of the illusion of control,
the hailing of economic formulae or virtue's principles.
Let us inhabit this solid universe,
where all we have is earth and soil,
fantasies fade to the airwaves
and we are just this, bone and blood,
bodies and beliefs,
the grit of here and right now.

Blessing

Bless with forgiveness this uncertain day.
Bless all who did their best,
face the night alone,
or in fickle company.
Bless all who fear the dark,
are consumed by guilt,
or dread the ghouls and ghosts of memories.
Bless all of us, the halt and blind,
this struggling band of ne'er-do-wells.
Let us unroll our sleeping mats,
the lame and lost,
and rest.

10:2

Waking

If dread crept into dreams,
or hearts broke with the dawn,
if morning came too soon,
or small hours slowly drawn,
then gently come the light,
and softly come the day,
smooth out this crumpled night,
wake peace in us, we pray.

Walking

Peace and justice: they pull against each other. My peace might be your injustice, my war your pax. It is like the bungees that secure a load to the roof of a car, these conflicting yet compatible concepts struggling to secure the luggage. Peace and justice are two good, moral devices that tension between themselves. Peace has a daily duel with justice. Whose peace do we desire and whose justice? Is my justice the same as yours? Is my peace at the expense of yours? We dance this dervish, spinning in whirls of desire and uncertainty. Both words sound good, but the tension between them can be overstretched.

Seeing

Stepping back,
looking at things differently,
sketching a line in the sand,
taking a deep breath,
giving benefit of the doubt,
taking all things into consideration,
offering another point of view,
being the devil's advocate,
on the other hand,
scanning things from all sides,
finding another way around,
walking a mile in another's shoes.

Acting

He said that she was being the "good cop" whilst someone else was playing "bad cop" and she said, "Don't be deceived by the good-cop act", and he laughed. He feels better for labelling her as "good cop", so that he can define what she does and what she says. But she says, she is not a cop, neither good nor bad, just trying to speak truth to power, to ask the seemingly daft question, to provoke the shallowness of the response and in her opinion, that's a fair cop.

Creating

It was like a tea urn with a tap at the bottom. They stood around whilst the beekeeper, in his suit and netted hood, approached with the flat slats of honeycomb still buzzing with the disturbed bees. They were allowed to view the sweet hexagonal wax-capped cells, oozing with golden liquid, before he inserted each one into the spinner. They took turns to rotate the handle and see the voluptuous, golden, sticky stream pour into the container below. Later there was a trophy of honeycomb in their empty lunchboxes to share at home. A childhood memory of buttered toast and sticky sweetness on fingers and chin, a gift from the bees.

Becoming

Angels don't flap, do they?
They pick up your post or water your geraniums,
or leave a casserole by the locked front door.
Angels don't fly around or boast.
Feet on the ground,
they pop by, drive you to the hospital,
or fall into step when you really need to talk.
Angels don't chorus incessant alleluias.
They lift the darkest gloom,
shade the candle flame,
sound lighter songs,
show you kindly how not to be afraid.
When you are doom laden,
night is all fright and grief,
they are nameless,
quite ordinary, actually.
Honestly, it is possible to miss them,
but they hang around anyway,
the heavenly host.

Reflecting

- When did we last meet an angel?
- How do justice and peace pull against each other?
- What childhood memories evoke a sense of peace for us?

Resting

The caterpillar has wrapped itself up and hung itself out like a sock on a twig washing line. I saw it making its way up the tree and now the job is done, the time of transformation has commenced. Inside that woolly coat it will break down into a juice and be reconfigured into a butterfly, providing no hungry bird decides it will make a tasty lunch. This process is complete risk, total disintegration. The waiting is not passive but rather the trusting of a mysterious process that is the only way it is going to get beautiful wings and fly.

Blessing

We kneel to praise you,
Creator of this most holy earth,
maker of the wide skies and fathomless seas,
the wide-armed mystery of love.
We kneel before you, penitent
for our angry hearts and warring spirits,
as you bring us to our knees in sorrow,
raise us to our feet as peacemakers,
peacekeepers, peacesharers.

10:3

Waking

In this day,
help me to match my aspirations with my actions,
be brave enough to stand up
against principalities and powers,
listen to those whose experience is different from mine,
believe in alternatives to violence.
Make my starting point, "equality".

Walking

To some she is "a Londoner", to others "a holiday-home owner", to others "an outsider", but she is also a neighbour, albeit intermittent and disruptive. She arrives at the holiday cottage like a tornado, rushing in having completed a week's work and driven north up the congested motorway. The locals brace themselves for noise and disruption as she sets about sorting the dust and cobwebs that have taken up residence in her absence. She plies them for gossip, trying to catch up as if she has been here all the time; they give her some headlines, but gossip has to be gossiped at the time and doesn't keep too well. She brushes the back path; she picks up the rubbish in the lane; she scurries around the garden snipping back the encroaching trees. And then she is gone, peace descends, and everyone breathes more easily again.

Seeing

In this day-to-day search for peace, I notice an ambivalence where those of us who aspire to such a high ideal soon revert to wanting a quiet life and those who have never known peace are subject to depression and fatigue. The need to re-orient ourselves, to dig deep, to keep going, to believe in a greater good than our own energies allow is a cost that is sometimes too burdensome to bear. Still, the remembering that we cannot and should not and need not do this alone holds a greater hope.

Acting

They called to mind the time there had been a man killing sex workers in the city where they both worked. First of all, there was the shock of it all, the sense of evil that someone would be so calculating and predatory. Then there was the need to be alongside people who were scared and vulnerable and to be a visible presence on the streets. Then there was the press, oh God, the press, hunting for some slant or angle that would make it seem as if this whole thing proved a point about the city. It seemed that the victims were somehow to blame: "They were no better than they should be." There were all those professional people who had worked with these women for months, years, who were rattled and angry.

Then they talked about what peace would look like, how these killings had shattered their sense of safety, but also how new bonds were found and how community development alone could not solve the issue. There needed to be new legislation about the purchase of crossbows.

Creating

Robert Louis Stevenson, troubled and lovelorn, travelled to Cevennes in the South of France to make a journey on foot with a recalcitrant donkey. He talked about coming down from the feather bed of civilization and travelling "not so much to go anywhere but to go". On his pilgrimage, he not only had to wrestle alone with the stubborn pack animal but also with his personal inner journey of discovery. He came to see that his narrow Protestant upbringing could be widened into new realities as he encountered the asylum of silence offered by the hospitality of Catholic monks. He described himself as an "inland castaway", and I wonder how we resonate with such a journey and how we can encourage the stubborn mule of our inner journeying to respond to the pocketed carrots of our onward imperatives.

Becoming

These things are so close together:
passion and anger,
resolve and stubbornness,
resilience and battling,
restlessness and temper.
Help me to walk the narrow path,
and when I don't,
help me to notice the detour
and adjust the compass.

Reflecting

- When have we noticed our inner journey has taken us to difficult places?
- Is there victim blaming in community development initiatives?
- Do we resist the struggle for peace in our longing for a quiet life?

Resting

When the river is cascading
with reckless crash
over the precipice of this day,
the rock face of every certainty
is slimed and slipping,
give me a momentary ledge
of solitude, I pray,
a small safe edge
behind the waterfall.

Blessing

Restore justice to this good earth,
strong hearts and right relations.
Bring peace to street and hearth,
Healing to heart and nations.

10:4

Waking

The waves of day,
cascade on the morning,
bringing salt breakers,
cleansing, stinging,
sucking away the silt and flotsam—
we stand, knee deep, unsure,
fearful of being overwhelmed,
consumed by forces that erode our certainties,
batter our defences, crumble fragile hopes to sand,
but tides turn,
tides always turn.

Walking

The *via negativa* suggests that we cannot say anything about God, only what God isn't, and I wonder whether this is also true of peace. We best surmise what peace means when it is absent, when there is violence or bullying or disquiet of the mind and we long for peace to return, yet it seems almost undefinable. Like love, peace seems as ethereal as mist, as elusive as a shadow, never to be grasped and held, only seen dancing enticingly on the edge of reality. And yet, somewhere within us, we continually

long for peace, strive towards it, imagine it to be possible. I
wonder why that is.

Seeing

She stood,
illumined by the light of her own meaning,
radiant in the crossbeams
of her enduring struggle.
She was a warrior, without a sword,
without a gun, without a bullet.
She was a fighter, without any means of defence
except the convictions of her own heart.
She was a heroine who spilled no one's blood
except her own.
She drew water from her own well,
tended the parched soil,
sowed the shrivelled seed,
believed the dusty ground would flourish,
carried the meagre vegetables to market,
fed her children,
was radiant,
in the simple light of her own meaning.

Acting

Give us courage to depose
all people who corrupt, corrode or plunder,
systems that loot, lift or pilfer,
evil masked as good intention,

self-interest colluding with inequality.
When we see these things in others
give us resolve to
recognize, resist and reconfigure them
in ourselves.

Creating

What is the place of the press in telling our story? We may look to journalists to recount and respin the narratives that surround us until we can get to a coherent world view, and yet there is such complexity in the human condition. The media, it seems, might relish conflict or dysfunction so that they can sell papers or increase internet traffic, but humans who live with daily struggles know that there is complexity and nuance in every story told. I wonder how we could not only remain informed about world events but also critique the stories we are being told. How can we be suspicious of the stereotypes with which we are presented in the echo chambers of our own internet profiles?

Becoming

Deepen me.
Dredge the deep sumps of
mossy silt that clog my soul,
that block the cross-stream's flow.
Scoop out the drift and dross of me,
make channels of clear water,
cleanse the dark depths of me,
sieve the salt and sandy rifts,
the hollow cliffs that falter me.
Keep sifting where doubt's quicksand sinks,
where I drift or dread and see
the silt, the bogs, the loss of me
and what I fear to know.

Reflecting

- How can we read behind the headlines to discover the depth of the stories we hear?
- Can we only define peace by what it isn't?
- Is strength the opposite of gentleness?

Resting

Where some sustain a sense of danger,
untangle my fear.
Where there is dread and apprehension,
calm my panic.
Enable me to rest within the story,
relinquish the headlines of imminent disasters.
Where there is paralysing danger,
be present and incarnate.
Let me be peace.

Blessing

Free me from the normal,
I pray.
Let me be eccentric and extraordinary
this day, I pray.
Let me rest in gracious hospitality
this day, every day, I pray.
Let me be unbound,
open to imagine
this gracious way, this day,
this holy day, this everyday,
I pray.

11:1

Waking

If the morning is uncertain,
unsure of our sexuality,
orientation, status, identity
in this white, hetero-normal, affluent place;
if we come out into the morning
with trepidation and anguish,
I pray that someone will listen and hear our stories.
As we long for recognition not just acceptance,
I hope that we will be seen
as glorious, beautiful, possibilities.
As life.

Walking

I have stepped through many darknesses to pause here under
this extravagant sky. I have travelled so much that my dreams
are haunted by loss of papers, missed flights, forgotten suitcases.
Now I stand under these frantic clouds and no longer envy
their urgency. There is peace here, in this stillness. There is
rootedness. There is connection to the dank soil, the smell of
the muddied ditch, the dew-wet berries. The gate is open and
invites me onward, but for now, this is home.

Seeing

The cemetery was beautifully kept by the Commonwealth War Graves Commission. Row upon row of upright stones, standing to attention with military precision. Here lie the bodies of over 6,000 soldiers who were killed in the Second World War, 52 who died in the First World War and a memorial to over 27,000 soldiers who died in the Burma Campaign and who have no known grave. Many of the soldiers are of the Indian Army and African regiments. On the memorial, in English, Hindi, Urdu, Gurmukhi and Burmese, are the words "They died for all free men".

Standing in this solemn place, I was mindful that this distant graveyard, some sixteen miles north of Yangon and some 6,000 miles from St Ives, linked this moment to my personal history. My father-in-law, son of a Cornish tin miner, had served in Burma with the Royal Berkshire regiment, and the stories he never told were as silent as these graves.

Most poignant were the graves marked "unknown", and it was only possible to conjecture about the pieces of shattered bodies that must have been bundled into this now well-watered earth. Whose families never knew what happened to their loved ones, when even their identifying dog tags had been "lost in action"

Years move on and, as Myanmar returns to military rule, the silence becomes audible once again.

Acting

There seem to be so few mechanisms for saying sorry, for admitting failure or mistake or oversight. There is always a legal or insurance or financial reason that this might be ill-advised. If the hospital could have admitted that her care had been remiss or the politicians that their strategies were flawed, then so much litigious anguish might have been avoided, a relationship established, a financial burden lifted, justice might have been enacted differently. Restorative justice is painstaking, compromise-ridden, unsatisfactory but ultimately, potentially holds a chance of lasting reconciliation and true forgiveness.

Becoming

I often ask God to do magic,
to hear my pleas and resolve my petitions.
I want God to wave a wand,
to conjure up solutions, to play the supernatural trump card.
But God is not Gandalf;
Jesus is not Merlin;
the Holy Spirit is not Tinkerbell.
Peace can only happen
by engagement, by love's presence in the here and now.
This is down-to-earth incarnation,
relational trinity.
This struggle is prayer.

Reflecting

Let the peace of Christ rule in your hearts, since as members of one body you were called to peace. *And be thankful.*

The reading from Colossians reminds us that the way of peacemaking is not only struggle but also joy. This is different from happiness; rather it is the deep knowledge that comes from searching for something more, something deeper, something eternal.

- How can we pray for peace in ways that are not wishful thinking?
- Where have we experienced silence becoming audible?
- When have we walked through many darknesses?

Resting

The eight-year-old asks her grandfather: "What do you want to do, fight a ninja chicken or a chicken ninja?" He thinks a while, as this is the three thousandth question of the day, and then he says, "I don't really want to fight anybody." For just a moment, there is quietness between them. He thinks that between the question and the answer there are about sixty years, sixty years of wanting to fight and be right, and knowing there is something better and coming to this place. He looks at her and ponders what the next sixty years will bring her, as the climate shifts and the virtual world creates bigger ninjas to fight stranger chickens. He suggests that she might like to run barefoot in the field outside, that she can get as muddy as she likes, that ninjas and chickens might not be the most important thing right now.

Blessing

Entice the people
to dare a radical way,
take a stand for righteousness,
embody peace.

11:2

Waking

When the dreams are too big for the night,
clouds too porous for the rain,
an overdraft of tasks
outspends the deficit of energy,
then restore hope in me,
hope replenished by creation's story,
birthed from darkness into
tentative yet glorious light.

Walking

What an opportunity for peace lies with the person who chairs a meeting! This seemingly mundane task holds a power so that everyone is heard and balanced decisions made. It is indeed a skill to get through a weighty agenda and enable people to "meet", to feel that their time together has been a constructive opportunity rather than a tedious chore. The agenda is never solely what is on the printed page but also emerges from previous conversations in corridors or car parks, past experiences or grievances. Remaining focused and clear, giving appropriate importance to the decisions that are crucial, enabling a detailed discussion without getting lost in minutiae, requires the skill of a surgeon and the wisdom of a sage!

Seeing

He was walking to the local shop, resentful that nobody else in the street was speaking English. The nice people said that he must resist racism, because there were only a small percentage of immigrants in the country as a whole. But this wasn't the country as a whole; this was his street and his corner shop that was now owned by Pakistanis. Once every person was white and spoke with the twang of a Yorkshire accent, not a different tongue. The nice people laughed and said, "The country hasn't been invaded", but this street and this shop and this place, where he once felt at home, felt as though they had been invaded and yes, it rattled him.

When he got back to the house, his neighbour Mr Mir was sitting in his garden. Before he could open his mouth in indignation, he noticed that his hedge had been trimmed. "I hope you don't mind, but I was doing my side and thought I might just as well finish the job," Mr Mir said with his broad Yorkshire accent. At the end of the day, whatever you thought about the others, Mr Mir was one of the best neighbours.

Acting

Economic development, financial justice and environmental pressures are so finely balanced in the peacemaking, peacekeeping process. When island communities take to their boats because of rising sea levels, when crops fail or invading forces steal land, then there is no option but to search for safety somewhere else. People move, migrate, flee in search of safety or security or identity. This fluidity of populations is a direct consequence of the changes in politics, economics or climate within which we all dwell. We know that we all have responsibilities to each other, yet we are often reluctant to share resources or land or prosperity. We need to live with less and view this as freedom, not a disadvantage, as a moral imperative not a hardship.

Creating

Between warmaker and the peacemaker
sling a rope bridge of understanding,
that each of them,
standing on the opposing escarpments
of their contradictory certainties,
might lean out towards each other
with reckless hope.

Becoming

We stand within this mystery, this exquisitely intense counterpoint of creation's longing for life and the seemingly inevitable entropy of death. We stand here, divinely wonderful yet painfully human; we stand dumbfounded by the pain and ecstasy, holding our pounding hearts and our aching chests. "God" is neither a big enough nor a small enough word for the expanse of this. We stand speechless in the profoundest of beauty and the torment of despair. We stand helpless and yet powerful, loved and yet desolate, hopeful, and yet perplexed. We seek answers but live only questions; we are terrified yet strangely courageous. We strive for a destination we can neither name nor own. Yet here we stand, and in the standing we become something authentic, something wise, someone true.

Reflecting

- How do we stand each day within our own contradictions?
- When have we had to confront our own racism?
- What would we need to change to live more thankfully?

Resting

He had been to a Christian festival. He had spent most of the day wishing he hadn't bothered. In his opinion, the music was too optimistically noisy, the conversations too self-consciously jolly, the speakers too earnest, the families too perfect. He was tired already of the contrived intensity and all the vicars in shorts. He stood at the gates of the campsite waiting for a taxi back to the hotel. The security guard came past with a torch, and they fell into conversation. The guard said that he did a lot of festivals and wondered about this one. He had noticed that there were a lot of families and not so many drunks as he was used to. For a while, they stood in the dark and chatted and curiously this conversation redeemed the day. It was OK to be on the edge, in the dark, away from the crowd, listening to the story of an ordinary bloke and his kids and his down-to-earth hopes.

Blessing

As a watchman standing at the gate,
as a mother waiting on the stairs,
as a lover listening for a text,
as a father pacing with a babe,
so may we, day by day,
step by step,
listen and long for love.

11:3

Waking

As dawn gifts light to darkness,
as moon stands aside for the sun,
so gift patience to anger,
fear stand aside for courage.

Walking

Hobbling, lame
we come, sore footed and blistered,
unheeled and unsoled
we cry out for attention.
See our need rolled out
like a prayer mat
beside this frenzied pool
of neglect and regret.
Hear us, forgive us, notice us,
call us out to leap and dance,
healed by the love of you,
living for the joy of you.

Seeing

In a room above a bookshop, a group of people are making bread. Before today, they did not know each other, but they are joined by the same task as they pull and stretch the dough with floury hands around the same table. Bread takes time to make, and as they engage in this simple yet demanding task, they talk and share stories.

The word "attention" has its roots in the Latin word *tendere*, "to stretch". To give somebody attention then is to stretch the space and time between them, so that there is a sense of being held in a liminal space, a betwixt-and-between place, in which all that matters is the other person and the immediate task in hand.

Around this table, the new bakers attend to each other and to the bread, and as they do so, their listening attentiveness not only stretches the dough, it also transforms their lives.

Acting

"Forgiveness" is not a command. We cannot even suggest it to someone wounded, even if the hurt was long ago. Even if secretly, we think that it is time to let go and move along. Forgiveness is not another burden with which to saddle those who are already hurting, another responsibility for a victim, another condition for recovery. Forgiveness is not a thing to be mustered from a traumatized soul or any kind of conditional reason for forgetting. If it happens at all, then it comes achingly slowly. If it comes at all, it is an unexpected, maybe unnoticed gift. If it comes at all it is not a condition on the victim's part.

Becoming

When she was first ordained, she was always referred to as a "woman minister", and she mused that nobody ever mentioned a "man minister", as if that was anything equally remarkable. Even her own mother asked her who would look after her children, as if this calling was somehow a dereliction of maternal duty. She replied: "We will", and there was a snort of resignation on the end of the phone. She lived a life of balancing and yet achievement, there was always a sense of "not as good as" that goes with being a woman and ordained. In the end, there was a triumph of the spirit, an understanding of self, an ever-present sense that the ordaining hands upon the head were authentic. She was surprised that some were frightened of her, as if they couldn't see the struggle and resolve that she had needed even to survive and that always she had to find another more tortuous route to the same destination.

Reflecting

- When have we been transformed by giving something our full attention?
- What questions could we ask to understand more deeply?
- How could we immerse ourselves in mischief and laughter but still be peacebearers?

Resting

Many ask "What?", and many ask "How?"
but few ask "Why?" or "Whom?"
"How?" and "What?" seek information.
"Why?" discloses soul and heart.
"Whom?" reveals the me and us.
To ask "Why?" and "Whom?"
brings understanding
to the bare facts of "What?" and "How?".

Blessing

Dove of peace,
baptize us
with strength and courage,
immerse us in
insight and resolve,
mischief and laughter.

11:4

Waking

Disorientated by waking in a different place my brain first asks, "Where is the bathroom?" and then, realizing that there might be no such thing as "a bathroom", consciousness cascades to a different question: "If there is no bathroom, where next?" Maybe our waking days are signposted by the location (or not) of a bathroom? I recall asking for the facilities in a village high up in the hills of Myanmar and being taken by a local woman up, up behind the shop, behind the dwellings, behind the chicken sheds and the meandering pig to a small shed with half a door and no lock. Staring into the abyss of the hole that served as a toilet, I was thankful for the half a door and the woman that stood outside. I realize that my need of privacy is a white, Western assumption I have no right to assume; I realize that privilege is written on the way I approach the world and the expectations I take to be normal. And with all that in mind, I am thankful to wake today in my own bed and proximate bathroom!

Becoming

He thought, as he had never been away from home before,
that he had never cooked anything at all, let alone an egg,
that the longer he boiled it, the softer it would get.
They laughed at him out loud,
unable to crack his bullet egg.
But in his defence
potatoes get softer, and lentils and meat,
and cabbage and stew,
they all get softer the longer you boil them,
so why would eggs be different?
To the point, what about humans?
The longer they are in hot water,
the longer they endure scorn,
the longer they get things ridiculously wrong,
do they get softer or harder?

Reflecting

- When did we last look into somebody's eyes and know them better?
- How do we decide when a risk is worth taking?
- Have we ever experienced "eloquent silence"?

Resting

He came out of his office frustrated that he had not cleared the surface of his desk, that there was no resolution or completion of the day. Laughing, she wondered why he would think that his desk would ever be cleared, why he would contemplate thinking that the day's business would be finished. He said that there was no way to know whether he had achieved anything; there was always a sense of incompleteness and unknowing about the day's events. She said, "Yep. Ain't that the truth."

Blessing

Into your hands,
gracious other, I commit my spirit,
into your spirit, gracious other,
I commit my hands.

12:1

Waking

We have worn each other out with wakefulness, and there is sand we cannot tip from our shoes; our hands are not sufficient to screen the glare from our eyes; everything is pivotal and vulnerable at sunrise. We squint into the light and perceive that peace is tentatively won from darkness.

Walking

We can consider walking as a safe, recreational, healthy activity, and mostly it is, but when people are murdered walking home alone after dark, the positivity is dispelled. It is hard to walk peaceably if violence is also prowling around. We become prone to walking defensively or avoid walking at all. Women are rightly annoyed when instructions to stay safe are applied to their perceived vulnerability rather than to the perpetrators of violence. It becomes apparent that there is a collective responsibility for both men and women to take strategies to keep each other safe and to be aware of each other's potential vulnerabilities and violence.

Seeing

Mostly we see what is nearest: the next task, the cobwebs in the corner of the kitchen, the need for reliable buses, our child's homework. But sometimes we see the whole thing, as if we were high above it all and able to dabble like a god high above this most beautiful and troubled world. In these moments, the solution is obvious: save the planet, start talking, love the ones that are gifted to us, resist the ridiculous squandering of war. In these moments of vision, when we can perceive how this troublesome world could resolve its differences, maybe when we feel most powerful, but ironically we are at our least powerful. Even so, this wide vision is crucial in showing us smaller things: campaigning for the rural bus service, being a school governor, seeing our kitchen as part of an ecosystem, loving more completely the ones that are gifted to us.

Acting

The project was called, "Weaving Women's Wisdom", and it simply invited women of any faith or none to gather around the common purpose of making a rug. They gathered, they garnered wool, material and memories to create a piece of canvas that told something of their stories. Colours, stitches, negotiations, contradictions all combined in the creative process, the outcome was unique and rich with colour, texture and narrative. The stories those mats held had to be heard and believed!

Creating

It was a grand piano, a fine Steinway, imposing and confident in its presence on the stage. The maestro pulled the seat forward and rested his delicate hands on the keys, intent on his performance with an inner world of harmonies and cadence ready to be shared with the audience hungry for the music of home. But this was not the Royal Festival Hall; it was not even the Sydney Opera House with an ambient temperature and a balanced atmosphere. Outside was the searing heat of the desert with its wide differentials between noonday scorch and night-time freeze. The piano was anarchic; it ached in its keys and pedals; it had expanded even since the piano tuner had settled its pitch, and now it was contracting with the cold night air. What was Mozart to say of this off-key rendition of a piece designed for the chambers of Strasbourg? Even this music was out of place here; the assembled and predominantly white community were patient, but, alongside the piano, they were reminded that they were strangers in the place.

Becoming

Peace will not come to me because I seek it, or because I pursue it, or aspire to it. Peace will only come alongside my striving for justice when I am actively challenging the dissonance of the world around me. Peace, then, is not a destination but a way of being, and by this, I mean that it is a way of being formed and honed and shaped by peace as an idea and an aspiration, as a possibility.

Reflecting

Let the peace of Christ rule in your hearts, since as
members of one body you were called to peace. And be
thankful.

The whole of the Colossians reading is calling us into transformation.
The rule of Christ is not simply a set of instructions to be obeyed
but a resolve to live differently and be formed in his likeness. As
the community who seek to "do peace", we will all be changed.

- How are we being shaped by peace?
- Where are the dissonances that need to be resolved?
- When can we be more attuned to each other's vulnerabilities
  and violence?

Resting

Into thy hands, I commend my spirit,
into thy wisdom, I commit my soul,
into your well of grace, I lob my unsettled self.
Into this turbulent whirlwind you call me to trust and hope,
call me into being,
call me into trusting,
call me into the calm of the storm's eye.

Blessing

Beloved, be loved.
Beholden, be held.

12:2

Waking

How has the dreaming found us sleeping in night's nest? Are our eyes shut dark, content in the depth of blue-black midnight? Does our bed fold us in an envelope of peaceful oblivion? How is the rebirth from darkness into light?

Walking

Peace is not always about resolving pain but being able to hold it in such a way that it doesn't destroy everything around it. He knew this because, as the priest, he heard of the accusations that were being brought by a young woman against her older brother. She said that there had been abuse, and this disclosure had blown the family apart. As he listened to the girl and the brother, the distraught mother and the angry father, this was not an easy place at all and yet his presence, just standing there in that family warzone, somehow brought a little peace.

Seeing

In the sheep trough in the Dale are a company of Water Boatmen who paddle about waiting to devour the insects that fall into the watery film. Held by the surface tension, they swim upside down. Whilst trying to photograph one, which was strangely difficult as the merest hint of a shadow caused them to dive, I was struck by the curious world view of a creature that swims upside down, and it made me ponder how often my world view is similarly inverted.

Acting

They made quilts. They took bits of old fabric, clothes, scraps, vintage items, offcuts, and from them they made the interlocking shapes. They worked as a group, discussing patterns, colour wheels, suitable edges; they were intent upon the task. Some were Muslim, others Christian and Buddhist; some had no faith but enjoyed the craft. They told stories of their journeys around the world or across town on a wet Thursday, as they stitched and ironed and formed the shapes.

This went on for weeks, and when it was finished they were both elated and disappointed. The quilt hummed with the music of their memories; it told stories of arrivals and departures, of hopes and depressions, of the weeks of being together in this way. The disappointment was that its finishing signalled a moving on to separate tasks, the common purpose complete. They had made a quilt, but that was just the beginning of a friendship too deep for words.

Creating

With a small amount of start-up money, the women were creating
vegetable gardens. The ground was powder dry, scorched by the
sun and eroded by the wind. Watering it was a constant task.
They scooped water with buckets and let it trickle onto the roots
of the plants as they bent over the rows. To start with they needed
to pull the water up from the well, which was backbreaking and
time consuming, but after a few years of growing, selling the
surplus produce from the patch, they had saved enough money
to buy a tank and a simple irrigation system. They kept careful
records and made sure that the profits were divided fairly. They
grew vegetables to feed their families and some cash crops for
the local market. They started to keep some livestock and use
the manure to fertilize the soil. This was not simply an activity
that led to the development of the land. It was also a means by
which they were more financially independent. With increasing
autonomy in the household, they were able to be more outspoken
against domestic violence and have a voice in local politics.

Becoming

The universe wills us
to inhabit the sodden acres of this
pained and fractured world,
stand on dark mountains,
descend unknown rifts and edges,
mixing with bog-sedge,
mires and peaty melancholy.
This is the soil from which we are formed,
from which we rise again.

Reflecting

- Where have we seen simple changes bring significant transformations?
- Have we ever viewed the world upside down?
- When has "standing there" been the only thing we could do?

Resting

Rest and peace are uncomfortable bed fellows. Rest implies a relinquishing of the daily stress, the sinking into "enough for now", the settee and the glass of Sauvignon. Peace, on the other hand, is an uncomfortable companion, always provoking a sense of incompleteness. In our quest for peace, there is always more to be done, so that we can never sink into complacency. How then to have rest and peace at the going down of the sun and in the morning?

Blessing

Bless the sinews, bones and tendons.
Bless the blood and binding.
Bless the body's aches and longings.
Bless the night's confiding.

12:3

Waking

We want to wake peacefully,
yet there is the drag and drift of yesterday,
anchoring us to darker deeps.
We want to wake bright-eyed and beautiful,
forgetting blisters, bothering,
past regrets.
We want to wake anew, joyous, dancing,
yet there is other grief, loss,
remorse, remembered troubles.
We want to wake differently,
yet here we are, all of this,
anyway.

Walking

Sometimes familiar words look very strange. This being the case, I am contemplating the word "monger". Meaning a peddler or purveyor (another funny word), it is usually associated with fish, cheese or iron or, as in the case of a costermonger, vegetables. As such, it is a fairly neutral word, except in relation to cheese, because clearly anyone that sells cheese needs immediate canonization for we all know that "Blessed are the cheesemakers!"

But when the word "monger" is attached to the word "war", then it takes a nasty turn, because a "warmonger" is somebody that deliberately and maliciously encourages rumour and violence along with an army of rumourmongers and scandalmongers.

What is the opposite of a warmonger? A peace peddler? This releases a subsidiary question because, whilst a warmonger trades in stirring up trouble, someone who is actively seeking peace is not trading in quite the same way, are they? We talk of positively promoting peace but that sounds more like an advert for something than a real something to be sold. We can change "peace" from a noun to a verb. We can aspire to peace in an ethereal way, but we can't purchase it or sell it.

So peace must be something to gift, to pursue, to generate, to proffer (yep, strange word!); peace, by ironic definition, must be free even though it is costly.

Seeing

Seeing and hearing are not separate senses. Truly to "see" another person, we need to listen deeply, to hear what is said in the gaps between the words, to hold them in our mind's eye. Listening is difficult: we are so often distracted by forming our own response that we tune out of what is being said to us. Listening is a whole-body activity, demanding focus. Only when we listen attentively to another person's story do we begin to have the insight to comprehend what they are saying.

Acting

When we first met him, the peacekeeper had been standing on the top of the steps on the narrow road that led from the market. He stood there most days, because it was the route that the children took to school, and he was watching over their safety. Too often they were harassed or called names, sometimes assaulted. We met him again as we drank coffee in an arched windowless room beside one of the city streets. He was a retired Australian schoolteacher, now wearing a flak jacket and peaked cap. He knew his presence was important, but he was finding the relentless threat of violence and the daily trauma to these young children challenging. He was also missing his own grandchildren back home. "Sometimes," he confided, "it all seems too hopeless and us being here just a pointless exercise, but then when the children smile at us on their way past or we see them chattering about ordinary things rather than walking silently with their heads bowed with fear, we think it all could be worth it."

Creating

Most people were out trekking in the mountains, wooed by the Himalayan experience and breathing the thin air of high altitude for the first time. She, on the other hand, was on a different mission, to find the weavers. She had made the acquaintance of a woman in a shop in the small town. The shop had bags and rugs, colourful purses and scarves. The woman told her that she was part of a cooperative of Tibetan refugees who were living in a small settlement out in the hills. She offered to take her there when her husband next went to collect the items for the shop.

The houses were ramshackle and simply made of corrugated iron. There were a few items of furniture and cooking pots. As the man negotiated the prices for the goods, she smiled at the children and communicated as best she could without a common language. The women had backstrap looms and sat on the front stoop with the warp stretching the length of the house and tied to a stick that stretched across the rear threshold. Inside the house, these taut threads were simply part of the household as children, dogs and grannies stepped over them in order to go about their daily business. On the front step, the women stretched backwards to keep the tension whilst throwing the simple shuttle to and fro.

After the visit, the woman in the shop explained how the cooperative worked. They were able to sell the goods to tourists at a profit, and this in turn allowed for hospital treatment and education in the refugee communities. Justice and peace are sisters, she said.

Becoming

Let me be peace,
let every part of me be peace.
Let me be presence,
let every part of me be presence.
Let me be still,
let every present part of me remain still.
Let me still remain present,
let every part of me remain present.
Let peace, presence, stillness
be who I am.

Reflecting

- When has trying to keep the peace seemed futile?
- Are justice and peace sisters?
- What is the opposite of a warmonger?

Resting

The graves gleam with a sort of peace,
leaning a little, sunken in parts,
they have settled for this.
On the other side of the fence
we are chopping up a fallen tree,
stilling the chainsaw as we
see a mourner with flowers,
silently conversing with an absence.
Quietly we pile the logs into the car,
to store for a season
and be winter-burned.
Carbon to carbon,
ashes to ashes,
dust to dust.

Blessing

If there is disquiet,
if there are echoes,
if there are shadows,
lighten them gently
with the rising moon,
with the watching stars,
with the patient candle.

12:4

Waking

Go!
It is the Mass,
sending you into this crumbling
bloodied world—
waking you to this new life
to share, to speak, to dare
as bread and dawn
have broken.
"Go!"

Walking

"Worry," he says, "is in the job description of being a parent."
Love and worry, after all, are two sides of the same coin; it is
not possible to have one without the other. There is always this
balancing between holding fast and letting go, between keeping
safe and letting free. "God knows," he says, "it's hard enough!"

Seeing

He had seen three peace walls. The first in Belfast, grey and sombre, slicing the city with a scar of graffiti and barbed wire. The second in Palestine, sometimes called a separation barrier or fence, demarcating different areas for different communities. Both times he heard the stories, saw the memorials, noticed the images and defiant words sprayed onto the surface, and both times he had an overwhelming sense of sadness.

Then he remembered, years ago, he had also seen other bits of wall, for sale in Germany as supposed mementoes of the Berlin Wall, now simply an historic curiosity for tourists. In remembering these fragments, his heart lifted slightly. It is possible for walls to crumble but only when they are renamed as atrocities, only when human relationships are so restored that separation walls are not deemed to be an essential safety mechanism. He mused that those barriers were always a sign of human failure, that they might reduce violence, but they never brought peace.

Acting

Washed ashore, having capsized or tumbled from boats, the refugees had nothing but the useless lifejacket and the blanket they were given when they landed. The lifejackets were often the cause of drowning rather than buoyancy, and they were glad to shed them on the beach. The blankets were rough but soon replaced by more serviceable clothing. Taking these two items and making them into strips the women began to weave mats. These were sold for a small profit, which meant they were able to afford to go to the local town for essential medical care and supplies.

Creating

The singers are coming from every state to gather in the centre of the country; they represent both indigenous and non-indigenous participants. There will be over 100 women, including many from Central Desert Aboriginal communities. The gathering gives the opportunity to share stories, to make relationships and to enjoy musical and cultural heritage. Music is the point for identities to meet, learning and singing together; as such it makes a sacred gathering, a rich and healing celebration.

Becoming

If only this friendship between the three of us
could extend around the table,
how we would draw our chairs closer,
talking, laughing,
disagreeing well.
How we would come together differently,
maybe reach right across the room,
the parliament, the world!
If only this amiable chinwag, this chewing of the cud
could be translated into the language
of debate, of conference, even of summit meeting.
If only we could stop othering the other,
be amenable to our differences,
name our truths gently.
If only peace could be the amniotic
fluid from which a new sort of conversation
could be born.

In Conclusion

Maybe it is only when we strive for peace, keep believing in its elusive possibility, set our face to its lightship across the stormy water of persistent conflict, when we consistently and resolutely reject violence in ourselves and others, when we determine that, despite all evidence to the contrary, peace can be achieved, maybe it is only in that striving and believing that peace will come, not as a completion but as a gift. Maybe peace really is a doing word.

Blessing

Imagine in us, we pray
a peaceful way.
Amen.

Ingram Content Group UK Ltd.
Milton Keynes UK
UKHW021406040523
421226UK00018B/58